To Helen!
Thank you for
your support)
Follow your heart!

From Heart to HRart

Empowering You to Work, Live, and Love

SAMM SMELTZER

Year of the Book

135 Glen Avenue

Glen Rock, PA 17327

ISBN 13: 978-1-945670-66-4

ISBN 10: 1-945670-66-5

Library of Congress Control Number: 2017961576

DEDICATION

This book is dedicated to my incredible husband, Josh Smeltzer, and my amazing best friend, MaryRose Higginbotham Ritter.

"Thanks for being my blanket, my shield, and ultimately my mirror for the good, the bad, the beautiful, the ugly, and all of those complicated gray areas in between."
~Michelle Zunter

It is because of your relentless love, support, and belief in me that this book was possible.

TABLE OF CONTENTS

PREFACE

For years, people have told me I should write a book. Honestly, I thought this was something people just say. I never gave it any serious consideration until I opened my business in 2014. Then writing became appealing because it was a way to establish credibility and build my business.

I quickly outlined half a dozen topics I routinely share with leaders, and thought writing the book would be easy-peasy. But every time I started a draft, I found my heart wasn't in it. I was knowledgeable about the subject and even great at teaching in the corporate training arena, yet when I would start to write, it lacked luster. This was going to be my first book and I wanted to be passionate and proud of it. So I stopped writing. Occasionally, I would attempt a different topic and outline, ending up in the same place. My heart still wasn't in it.

In 2017, I was invited to attend an evening event showcasing local authors. These amazing women shared their stories in a panel discussion led by their writing coach and publisher, Demi Stevens. Demi shared that we all have a story to tell and that she has devoted her career to helping get that story from your head to the page. I connected with her after the panel discussion and she encouraged me to reach out—of course I never did.

A few months later, my friend and colleague, Amanda King, announced the release of her book, *HR Made Simple*—and guess who was her publisher and writing coach? *Demi*. Seeing Amanda share this amazing accomplishment was the last push I needed to finally take the next step.

I went to Demi with no outline, just a bunch of random writings... stories I felt compelled to share. I had no idea how they related to each other, but I knew they were meant to be in this book. I could now feel it in my heart.

This book is just that—my heart exposed.

As you read, I hope you find that nudge needed to move you forward to the next great thing in your life. I hope to inspire you to move past fear and heal wounds of past hurt. I hope you recognize the beauty in the lessons of life, whether they are full of joy or difficulty. I hope you grow, become stronger, and more aware. Most importantly, I hope you enjoy it.

The Organization

This book is separated into two parts. Part One is my heart exposed to you, containing all the stories I felt compelled to share. They are my account of what I have experienced and my growth as a result. In addition, I throw a few nuggets of wisdom from minor bunny trails where I simply couldn't help myself.

Part Two is all about exposing your heart. These chapters are shorter, and articulate five major lessons that can be derived from the stories shared in Part One. Each chapter ends with a corresponding experiential exercise to get you started in doing some heart work.

My recommendation is start with Part One and do not jump to Part Two, as tempting as it may be. We always want to go directly to action without fully understanding the why first. If Part One does not resonate with you, Part Two isn't going to either. So without further ado, let's get started with Exposing Me before we even consider Exposing You.

PART ONE

EXPOSING ME

INTRODUCTION

I was invigorated once again. It was becoming a trend... about every three years I needed something new. Perhaps that's why I felt like I kept hitting dead ends. Maybe I should have picked up on it sooner that the three-year mark was inevitably the start of some very self sabotaging behaviors – behaviors that ultimately created a self-fulfilling prophecy of unhappiness.

The unfortunate thing is that it was not only me along for this ride. I also brought my completely devoted husband and two beautiful little girls, though at the specific moment where the story begins, there was only one beautiful little girl.

This was the true beginning of everything, and it started with invigoration...

AS GOOD AS IT GETS

You see, at this point in my life, I had made a few conclusions. First, I highly doubted my life could ever be anything more than it already was. Second, (which is a complete contradiction) I realized my drive and need for *more* was part of who I am, a mere personality trait.

This time, my *more* had materialized as yet another direct sales venture. Previously, I had given the romance adult industry a try. Convinced that would be profitable – since obviously "sex sells" – I did this for a number of years without many people in my life knowing. I did okay, but honestly, I think I got more entertainment out of it than compensation. This time, my direct sales opportunity was personalized bags—something I could tell everyone about. I mean, if I had been mildly successful in a business I shared with practically no one, I had the potential to be wildly successful with a product I could share with everyone.

And let me tell you, I was all in. I invested in inventory and samples. I listened to all the conference training calls. I completed all the challenges. I worked trade shows every weekend. I even splurged to attend the national conference in Nashville... all while maintaining full-time employment and finishing my graduate degree.

In case you're curious, let's reveal the mystery of my day job. I worked as a full-time corporate trainer whose focus was Staff Development. Appropriately, the graduate degree I was pursuing was a Masters of Education in Training and Development. I was all in on that job, too. *All in*, but not satisfied. It wasn't enough.

The fact that I was lacking fulfilment was a mystery to me. I had worked hard to get where I was, and had pretty much marked off all the boxes on the checklist of dream job. My full-time position was filled with responsibilities that allowed me to do exactly what I loved. Gone were the generalized HR jobs where only a small percentage of the time was work that fulfilled me. Gone were the positions dominated by that horrible phrase – *other duties as assigned.*

I worked 36 hours per week and my pay was equal to my previous job working 40+. My office was a 15-minute commute from home, and Fridays were typically half-days. Plus my boss was the whole reason I wanted to work there in the first place.

We spend our lives working, almost a total of 90,000 hours, but it is important to realize work is not our life.

Now don't get me wrong. The position wasn't perfect, but the circumstances were pretty darn close. That's why I was so perplexed when I still felt incredibly unsatisfied, which led me to believe that perhaps this was "as good as it gets" and I would have to find other ways to add satisfaction to my life... because clearly career alone was not sufficient.

Mine vs. Theirs

I'm telling you this because it's where it all started. This was the first time I saw life for what it is – a fork in the road. The power of free will is an incredible gift that empowers us to be happy. But so many of us, myself included, are afraid. Therefore, we veer left instead of right, heading down a path that feels so comforting at first, but routinely ends with the most uncomfortable moments – moments we'll label as *mistakes* or *failures*—that make us believe less in our worthiness and ability to be happy.

I can firmly tell you this. We all have a purpose. We all are living and breathing on this earth in this life for a reason. Your purpose can be as grand as sharing a message to millions, but it can also be as powerful as changing one person's life through something smaller. We are here together to help each other get to that place we desire, whether we blatantly put it out there, or hide behind denial. We are all searching to find where we fit in this massive puzzle of life.

But initially, seeking out comfort is like allowing someone else to make the decisions for you. It is choosing to give up our gift of free will and say to the universe that others know us better than we know ourselves.

Perhaps this feels familiar. Maybe you've traveled to the end of this path before, where you become heartbroken when you learn those other people don't know you at all. Then you become angry because you believe they want you to change, and that you're not good enough.

The truth is they don't know you.
They can't know you... because
you don't know yourself.

Until we know ourselves, then and only then can we share it with the world. No one will ever know what you know inside, what resonates within your soul and vibrates to your core. You have to allow yourself to choose the "right" path, and to choose it for yourself.

This is the story of my realization, noticing that I kept veering down the "left" path, refusing to look inside, and as a result achieving only the success of what others defined for me. A good life... that lacked serious fulfillment.

PERMISSION GRANTED

One day I received an email from this new direct sales venture company of mine. It proudly shared their recent recognition for being top in their industry for training. The light bulb went off for me – I connected that my day job and side passion could mutually benefit each other. It was the only permission I needed to allow my two jobs to begin intermingling.

This permission equated to allowing myself to browse their website during working hours. I justified it by saying it was research to see what resources I could utilize to benefit my primary organization. *Duh.* This sequence of events, however, was the only reason I ever gave a real look at their book club.

By default, I do not identify as an avid reader, and I was already overwhelmed by the amount of reading required for my graduate classes. Therefore, believe me when I say I would never have actively sought out or considered additional reading opportunities. When the direct sales company first introduced their book club, I flat out completely ignored it.

Their first selection was a book called *The Slight Edge*, by Jeff Olson. I had never heard of it, so I did a little research. It was the story behind the book that most intrigued me. The author was just your typical successful guy. (By *typical* I mean he had a similar resume to countless other authors with life-changing advice on how you can be just like them.) But what got me about Jeff was that his intention was never to write a book. He was only sharing advice and stories that friends and colleagues were already asking about. If anything, the book became a vehicle to make the sharing process more efficient, effective, and powerful.

The Slight Edge and its contents in raw form produced changes and success stories almost instantly, catapulting the book to its current throne as royalty in a long line of self-help books. It has also become known as the prerequisite for self-help books, equipping you with the foundation necessary to benefit from all the other bestselling self-help books, and to apply those skills to your life.

THIS WAS NOT MY INTENTION

Similarly, it was never my intention to write a book. However, as I continue to travel down the "right" path, I have been guided to many who find themselves on their "left" path, struggling to cling to the hope that a purpose for them exists. I am no different than these individuals. I walked the same path as they did for most of my life. In fact, I am still a victim of self-sabotaging habits established over the decades. Still today, I must live my life intentionally to ensure I keep moving forward.

It seemed that I felt compelled to share the same stories and lessons routinely with friends, family, and clients. These stories and lessons of my healing seemed to aid others in their need for healing. Just as *The Slight Edge* gave Jeff Olson the opportunity to craft a more effective message that could be universally delivered, that is what I hope to achieve with *From Heart to HRart*. This is my universal message of internal transformation to happiness, as cheesy as that may sound. But don't we all want a little bit of the cheese sauce?

THE SLIGHT EDGE

When I received Jeff Olson's book, it was a simple paperback, no fancy cover. The outside was white with the title printed in blue. That was it. Casually flipping through the book, there were a few simplistic diagrams, but nothing too complicated. I started to read casually and then quickly found myself swept away.

It was intoxicating, like someone was reading my mind. My thoughts were being displayed right in front of me in words. Jeff's stories – although different than mine – resonated at a level within that I rarely showed to the world for fear of judgment.

I often tell people that if common sense existed, Jeff's book would be it. Its contents are primarily what we assume people already know, and what we expect to see, especially in a professional context. However, this book changed my career, and I would like to think bringing it to my day job allowed that book to change other's careers as well. But what I didn't know was that it would do much more for me than become a great training tool to share with the world. The principles Jeff Olson taught were coming alive in my life.

The Slight Edge discusses the power of time. Jeff shares that time has the ability to either promote us or expose us. The trick is that we have no idea when either of these things will occur. So we basically have only one option: we cannot control time, but we can choose every day to make decisions that make time work for us... or against us. The sad thing is, most of us (myself included) choose to pay no attention at all. Time continues and the turning point moves closer and closer until one day we wake up and realize we've been exposed completely.

*Every decision affects your life—
what you say, and what you don't say...
where you go, and where you don't go...
and yes, even what you do
and do not choose to eat.*

In 2014, time began to expose me, and this book is the story of the most powerful and vulnerable moments it delivered. Now years later, I can finally look back and see it for what it was. The curve of life coming alive, and I had no idea which way it was curving, up or down, towards success or crashing into failure. I felt like I lost all control, like time had taken over and all my decisions had caught up to me.

THE CANVAS

My exposure moments are average in the grand scale of the world. However, the vulnerability was monumental and transformational for me. My journey includes both my climb and my ultimate fall back to a blank canvas. It is through this blank canvas, I realized I am the artist, and whatever I want is the possible outcome. I can pick the colors rather than try to force myself to like what others have selected for me.

This canvas is available to each of us and has been waiting since we first came into this world. It's just that we live with so much junk put on us by other people, intentionally and not, that we quickly forget we are the artists of our own lives. We forget we have a path of our own... a purpose of our own. We merely become part of a world that has forgotten and is terribly lost.

I hope by sharing my path of healing, essentially reconnecting with my originally intended path, that it will inspire you to pursue your own.

CHAPTER 1

FROM COMFORTING TO VERY UNCOMFORTABLE

"I want you to push through the comfort and get uncomfortable," my trainer said. I was standing on an indoor turf that was 30 yards long, in front of a sled weighing more than 150 pounds. Shortly, I would be expected to pull that same sled for 30 yards and then push it another 30 yards, and then repeat this for 4 rounds.

The idea that I could actually be comfortable doing such an action seemed like nonsense. A year before when I had started this training, I clearly recall never feeling an ounce of comfort. The entire working-out/getting-stronger process was uncomfortable... and sometimes even painful.

I knew the comforts my personal trainer referred to were the times I would stop and rest—usually at about the 15-yard mark during my rounds. I did so to pace myself and maintain rhythmic breathing. I have aerobic-induced asthma, and if I've learned anything it's knowing which exercises quickly trigger my symptoms and can jolt an attack. But even saying that to myself felt like I was making excuses. Clearly, the comment put my thoughts on defensive... and from my point of reasoning it was completely justified.

Now let me explain why I had a personal trainer in my life, because it illustrates even more so why this concept of being comfortable is ridiculous. See, when I look in the mirror, I see a woman who is not beautiful, or even attractive. The mere consideration of being *sexy* makes me chuckle. If anything, I'm cute, adorable and chubby.

This struggle to see outward beauty in myself is new. I can't say I have had to deal with it my whole life. Then again, I can't exactly say I haven't.

Sammi Baby

Sammi, Sam, Samantha... these are the names I responded to when I was a child. Growing up in sunny California, my mother would call me *Sammi Baby*, and my father simply *Sam*. *Samantha* was reserved for times when I was in trouble, or for my grandmother who believed that *Sam* was not a suitable name for a girl.

I was a happy child, full of life and energy. I was also full of dreams. I would play school and house, but my favorite thing was to pretend to be a rock star. I would belt out songs I thought only I could hear, though I now know several others were listening. Music was a true place of joy for me, and I dreamed of creating my own songs and being on stage to share them with others. What I didn't fully understand at the time was the amount of vulnerability that musical performance encompassed.

Fear often paralyzed me, and therefore my creations were doodled solely in journals or childhood diaries complete with locks. They were sung in backyards while I played by myself, and on a mock stage in our living room with no one watching. Music was a dream I kept silent for many years.

My parents believed it was just a hobby and had no idea about my deep love for music. I connected with the songs. Music somehow made my life more vibrant. I'd had no lessons, and no real exposure or access to instruments, so I relied on the only instrument I possessed – my voice. But even then, I'm sure it sounded one way inside my head and completely different to others outside.

When I slowly began to let people in on my dream, their reaction confirmed that my vocal instrument was nothing special. I was not a Whitney Houston or Mariah Carey waiting to be discovered. I was not that type of special or unique.

As I faced this realization, I began to shift my energy to what I could actually attain.

What do you do when the thing you really want isn't an option, and the dream you've been dreaming all your life has to stay just that... a dream?

Was it really impossible? As children we are told we can achieve anything. When exactly does that possibility disappear?

I guess for me, it was at this point, and the reason why it disappeared was because I let others define what I was capable of. I was afraid, and I thought that challenging their judgment of me was an impossible task... and one I was not willing to take on.

AT LEAST I WAS BEAUTIFUL

The one thing I did have in my youth that worked in favor of a singing career was that I was nice to look at. My mother taught me from a young age, and instilled in me that I was just that – beautiful. And I would only become more beautiful with age. I am half Filipino and the other half German and Irish. In Filipino culture, mixed-race girls or women are called *mastisa* and it is commonly said that means you are going to be beautiful.

What a high expectation... to always be beautiful!

Beauty comes with benefits as well as a lot of unwanted attention. Even though I was pretty, I remember that I never received the attention from people who I actually wanted to notice me. Instead it came from people I had no interest in receiving attention from—catcalls while walking down the street, vulgar statements about what they wanted or could do for me... or to me. I was barely a teen and I was afraid.

All that attention made me nervous. Even my father was not pleased when it happened. This stuck out to me particularly because he never showed much emotion except in extreme circumstances. He traveled a lot when I was young, and then when he did eventually work from home, he worked in an office attached to our garage in the backyard and still treated it like a normal 8 to 5.

He would wake up and get ready to head to the office. Even though he was "home" he was rarely seen. Maybe around lunchtime he would make a brief appearance to make us lunch, or for the occasional bathroom break. But that was it. My interaction with him back then was limited. Even when he was around, we didn't talk much. The organic atmosphere was uncomfortable. He may have been merely feet away, but really it felt like miles.

That relationship has been completely transformed today. But to have my father visibly react and be disgusted by men making comments toward his daughter was expected. It was also unexpected at the time for my father and how I knew him.

The unwanted attention became a normal occurrence and I prepared myself to deal with it whenever I went out. Sometimes I would choose to not go out at all… to avoid the potential scenario… or when I did go out, I preferred to not be alone.

Then one day it went too far for me. Due to my parent's work schedule I had to start walking home. The private school I attended did not have school buses, and since my house was only a mile away, this made public transportation more of a hassle than it was worth.

When I first started walking home, it was no big deal because my brother was with me. But then he transferred schools and I was left to walk alone. In addition, because I attended private school, there were mandatory uniforms. I will never understand how an outfit so ugly somehow makes a girl more attractive.

My path home was along main roads with lots of traffic. This was the primary reason my parents felt okay with allowing us to walk home. The roads were very public, so the likelihood of abduction would be less. Right?

It was just another normal school day and I was walking home as usual. I would distract myself by singing random lyrics and melodies that I had made up – going to my imaginary world within my head where I was starring in my own music video, and they were filming me singing while I casually walked down the street. It is safe to say that I was in my own world. Which is sad, because that means I have no idea when the stalking actually started. I just remember this particular day because the individual did something that caught my eye.

The car was driving slower than the flow of traffic. It was a pale, sea-green Ford Taurus, an older model with rounded edges. I still jump when I see one. It caught my eye because it was moving slowly, like maybe something else had happened around me that

I should be paying attention to, perhaps an accident or something.

Upon further examination though, everything was as it should be, so I shrugged my shoulders and wondered if the driver was lost or old. Then I caught a glimpse of the same car, again driving slowly, and heading in the same direction as me... almost like déjà vu. The car passed me and I remember the sinking feeling in my stomach, like something bad was about to happen. But the car disappeared into the distance and didn't come by again.

The next day, about halfway home, I spotted the car again, driving a similar slow speed. Then it passed me again, and again... and again.

I was within three blocks of my house when it finally disappeared and did not return. That night I casually said something to my mother, who told me I was paranoid and probably a bit egotistical to think that I was worthy of being stalked.

For the next few weeks this became a semi-regular occurrence. The car would show up at about the same point and drive by several times. Then it would disappear, always before I got anywhere near my house, which made me feel somewhat safe since whoever it was didn't know where I lived.

I had also come to the conclusion that the driver wasn't doing anything but driving a bit slower. What harm was he really causing? I began to believe it was simply part of my normal routine. I never saw the driver as the windows were tinted just enough to blur the view, but I could see the person wore a baseball cap.

The following few weeks the mystery man started showing up a bit earlier in my walk and was more blatant about his circling pattern. He would drive up two or three blocks before turning and looping back to pass by again. Soon he began circling at every block and his drivebys became even slower. Sometimes almost a crawl. If a car approached from behind he would speed up and then circle again, but would always disappear before I was anywhere near my house.

Then one day amidst the circling, he slowed to a stop and pulled his vehicle over. I heard the car door open and a male voice casually say, "Hey."

A loud voice inside my head yelled, *"RUN!"*

I didn't look back and I didn't question the voice. I just took off as fast as I could. I darted down a street off my path and then ran through yards. I ran in every direction but the direction of home. The one thing I was certain of was that I didn't want this person to know where I lived.

After the adrenaline died down, I looked around but didn't see the pale, sea-green Taurus anywhere. I caught my breath and finally made my way home. Upon arrival, I didn't say anything to my brother, and I even highly questioned whether I should say anything to my mother.

That night when she got home, I did say something. Her response was not much different from her previous admonishment, and affirmed that the only important thing was that I was fine and that nothing happened to me.

Now today as a parent, I can only begin to imagine the different circumstances surrounding my mother and father at that time. We lived in beautiful Los Angeles, California, in one of the most expensive cities in the U.S. It was not possible to be a one-income family. My parents had decent steady jobs that required a minimum commute of an hour both ways. Afterschool childcare was neither practical nor necessary with me in eighth grade. Plus, I believed I was already an adult. I would've resisted. It's scary to remember how invincible I thought I was. This whole incident was humbling and a reminder that I was very much still a child with no true concept of the world we lived in.

THE DAY AFTER

At the time, I couldn't help it. I started to blame myself, thinking maybe I'd brought this upon myself. I was too pretty, or maybe I had worn my skirt too short. I was asking to be followed, taunting them to try something.

For the next few days, I took alternative paths home and when I finally resumed my normal walk I never saw that car again. Despite realizing the perpetrator had given up, I was still left with an internal feeling of helplessness and a deep-rooted fear of what might happen the next time.

Did I want to continue living as a walking, talking temptation, to see who would next pursue me?

When I started high school, I selected an all-girls private school, much farther away than my previous school. I was left with no choice but to use public transportation, or else not get home. Riding L.A. County Public Transit provided me with a whole wealth of new unwanted attention. This served as further assurance that I didn't want to be pretty anymore.

I mean, the only true benefit of being attractive was to help my singing career, which everyone had made perfectly clear was not going to happen, so why should I stay beautiful? To find a man? No, thank you. I would be perfectly content without one.

This marked the beginning of a practice that would be extremely indicative of what was to come for me. Every day I stopped at the Savon Foods (a local convenience store) by my house. I would save just enough from my lunch money to buy a king-sized Snickers bar to eat during my last few blocks home.

Now sure, a king-sized candy bar won't kill you or make you immediately fat, but one a day over a year will begin to take a toll. That success was confirmed by my father just before our family made a cross-country move to Pennsylvania.

MY FIRST LESSON IN EXPOSURE

Have you ever been in a training session or attended a presentation and listened to the speaker's examples, thinking *"How silly, that would never happen"*? These examples usually get a chuckle from the audience because they sound completely unrealistic. Well, when I first brought *The Slight Edge* philosophies into my classroom and shared the concept of time promoting and exposing us, the example I pointed to was my decision to eat a king-sized Snickers candy bar every day. Because one day, time exposes our habit and someone is going to call us out on it.

It was a normal day, at home, and everyone was doing their thing. My father and mother were out in the backyard casually conversing as always. I was inside the house going about my business, when I needed to make a pit stop at the restroom. The bathroom was at the back of the house and its window was always cracked open to let the California sunshine and air in. Not only did it let in sunshine and air, but also it carried backyard conversations like a microphone.

My parents had made the decision that we would be relocating across the country to Pennsylvania. The transition would take about a year because they didn't want to pull me or my brother out of school midway through the year. So the topic of moving and transition was a popular one, but in this conversation I heard my father say...

"I hope when we get there that Samm gets more active again. She's starting to put on some weight."

A hurt, shocked, and hormonal 14 year old, I simply yelled out the window, "I can hear you, you know!"

There was never any follow-up to that comment. My family carried on as if nothing had happened. I mean, I wasn't surprised, but that day I went from *beautiful* to *bigger*. I was a size 5.

When we moved to Pennsylvania, I didn't get more active. In fact it went in the polar opposite direction. At the age of 15, I felt alone and so I isolated myself accordingly. On the rare occasion that I did venture out, I discovered that the food selection was very different. Instead of smoothie and trendy coffee shops to hang out at, there were annual fairs and small-town diners full of fried foods loaded with butter.

After a cross-country plane ride, the equation of my life went from:

ACTIVE + FEEL GOOD FOOD = BEAUTIFUL

to

NO ACTIVITY + FRIED FOOD = BIGGER

In that first year alone, I went from a size 5 to a size 9, and the comments regarding the growth of my waistband increased. Coincidentally, the comments were not coming from those I was befriending, but from those whom I loved and treasured the most.

The Return of the Closet Dream

I decided to enter college to pursue music. My closet dream was clearly out now, but only partially exposed. Due to paralyzing fear, I never let anyone see quite exactly what music meant to me. Nevertheless, I did at least get myself to the point of trying.

I spent the last two years of high school immersed in accelerated music lessons in hopes that I could pass the basic audition levels required for admission. I also picked a music school in the middle of nowhere. This seemed contradictory since the culture shock of small-town York, Pennsylvania, had still not worn off. I could have gone back to sunny California, but instead I stayed, choosing this particular school out of comfort.

I had made up an elaborate story inside my head that if I pursued music in a little town that the competition would be less, and as a result it would increase the likelihood of my dream actually coming true. But this was quickly proven wrong on audition day at campus. While we were sent to a long row of tiny rooms containing nothing more than a piano and stool. I sat there at the piano alone with my mother and around me I heard some of the most beautiful voices warming up and running scales. I began to hyperventilate. I couldn't calm myself. What was I doing there? I didn't belong there. Needless to say I didn't warm up before my audition, I instead attempted to calm myself enough just so I could sing and hopefully not go flat or sharp. I was so nervous it was almost paralyzing. My mother attempted to reassure that I had some sort of talent, making me feel deserving to be there. But this cheerleading was coming from someone who used to laugh at my dream.

I made it through the audition. Not perfect by any means. I forgot the words to my second song, but managed to do a bouncing staccato *um* to the notes almost perfectly. And after the day was over, I was told they were going to accept me. This college in a small, small town was going to allow me to pursue a degree in Music with elective studies in Business. To me, business was a safety net, in case I truly couldn't sing or wasn't good enough as a performer, that maybe I could find somewhere to be in the magical world of music business. Be a part of it in some way. It truly is all I have ever wanted or dreamed of.

The reality of music education set in very quickly. The necessary amounts of time needed to dedicate to practicing tripled for me since I had the least amount of formal training. Most of my peers had been studying their instruments since early childhood. I was still terrified and tried to find a practice time when the music building was not so populated... so I could practice without fear of being mortified. *If only the practice rooms were soundproof.*

I struggled in all my classes. It was a mixture of intimidation and just having a lower foundation of training than the others. I even took some remedial music classes which I actually did pretty good in, so that gave me hope. Despite the large amount of apprehension that I still harbored, deep down it was pure joy that warmed my heart... to finally be in a place pursuing my dream.

As far as socially, I cliqued with a few of my peers but not really. Instead I developed most of my close friends outside the music program. I was looking for some sort of comforting distraction outside my academic career – someplace where I didn't feel "not good enough." The few students who I did click with, didn't stay very long and eventually dropped out after the first few semesters. Despite all my struggles, I was passing, even if barely and for a while it all seemed possible. I could graduate with a Music degree as a vocal major.

Then came the Sight Singing. Every test was a repeat of audition day. They should teach Nervous Nellie 101. It didn't matter how much I practiced, on test day I became paralyzed with terror and my singing became erratic and not in tune or on rhythm. I didn't fail but I received the equivalent, a "D," which was not passing in the requirements for my degree. I took the class twice, receiving the same grade both times. It was then that I knew I couldn't do this.

RUNAWAY

I had a decision to make: continue to attempt to pass Sight Singing I... and then later attempt to pass Sight Singing II, III and IV. If I chose this path, I knew I would have to kiss goodbye any graduation date expectation. I would have to focus on trying, practicing and never giving up. But the fear was there whispering to me, *"What if you just can't do it? What if you take an extra two years and still don't pass? What if you waste all that money only to discover what you already knew – you can't do it. You're not good enough."*

I decided to meet with the registrar and asked what other degree programs would take most of my current credits. I wanted to know what my options were that would set me back the least, since I obviously was already set back. Two programs were possible, which would only result in one extra year for me to complete a degree. And I was going to get a degree. I had already spent too much time and too much money. I needed something to show for all that debt I would be paying back over the rest of my life.

The fact that my current program had a minor in business meant all those credits would transfer. My vast music credits would simply populate and meet all elective degree requirements. My choices were a Bachelor of Science in Marketing, or Management. My experience around campus showed that the Marketing program was a large one with a lot of people. On some days it seemed like everyone was a Marketing major. That brought to mind feelings once again of competition and I wasn't ready to lose again. Therefore, I defaulted to Management and my college career became less of an experience and more of a checklist.

As for singing, I stopped all together. My vocal teacher encouraged me not to give up, but I was beyond traumatized. The idea of ever exposing myself like that again was unbearable. In addition, the extra year of schooling I needed meant I couldn't afford the lessons, or the time. Being proactive, I started the process of transferring to York College and planned to move home. This was the final step to officially end my so-called college life. Any relationships I had established were left behind, only to return to a city where I barely had any friends to start with.

When I arrived at York College I had one objective: pass every class and get the degree. I had been working at the local Home Improvement Store during the summers and now that I was back home I could work with them year-round. I increased my hours as well, since I didn't really have anything else to do besides school. Quickly I became a full-time student with pretty much a full-time job, and I lived simply going through the motions.

MOMENTS OF DISCOMFORT

If you didn't feel uncomfortable reading that scenario, I want you to know that living it was extremely uncomfortable. If we were to go back to the philosophies shared in *The Slight Edge* we'd learn that actions which begin in discomfort eventually transform to a place of comfort. This is an attribute typically associated with an upward curve or success curve.

However, when these moments lessened in discomfort for me, the transformation to comfort was a sort of contradiction. Though I was successful by definition to an outward world, inside I felt a long way from my personal definition of success. The story of going from discomfort to comfort, for me, was much more like from Beauty to Beast.

- -

EXPOSED IN THIS CHAPTER:

1. The concept of being comfortable can be ridiculous.
2. As children we are told we can achieve anything. When exactly does that possibility disappear?
3. Unrealistic stories that easily get a chuckle may hold a very uncomfortable truth.
4. Fear whispers can be the sole cause for a massive detour.
5. Your personal definition of success is what actually matters.

- -

CHAPTER 2

GOODBYE BEAUTY, HELLO BEAST

It's important to realize that my current professional industry chose me. Seriously, I switched degrees to a concentration in Management and I intended to take it literally. That meant finding a job in management, and since I already had a semi-established career in retail, I thought, why not become a retail manager?

Apparently, that was not in the stars for me. A sequence of events was about to occur which would put me on a path I didn't even know existed. The first event happened in an employee break room while I was eating my lunch.

It was in this moment that I first noticed the trend. Or maybe a better description would be common practice, regarding a break room ritual. This routine is not unique to this particular break room. As I watched the people who came and went to their lockers preparing for their work day or finishing up to head home, I noticed the faces of many carried a heavy burden of unhappiness and dissatisfaction. And if you listened to their words and heavy sighs, it only confirmed this misery.

I'm often reminded of this heaviness, this burden of unhappiness, when I talk with someone who has found themselves in a place of life that they least expected.

In that moment when I first became aware, I couldn't help but fear it might be me ten years down the road, or maybe even just one year later. There was no way I could guarantee that I was on the right path. I mean, I had just decided to leave my life dream behind. I was aimlessly going where the wind blew me, but on this day it blew me into that break room and made me pay attention. Feeling helpless and somewhat apprehensive of what the future might hold for me, I sought out what I could control. I started to ask questions.

We all grow up expecting to work for the majority of our lives, but if we are unable to do what we dreamed of as children, couldn't we at least be happy? Why can't those who are going to employ us care? Care about their employees, the people who are there to help them achieve their dream? That is what I couldn't understand. In a world where someone is able to achieve their dream, someone who somehow found the path to make it possible... would they not care for those who support their dream, without whom their path would be impossible?

This is when I discovered what that little office in the corner with the name "Human Resources" was for. Their true purpose was much more than hiring, training, and benefits. They were present to be a voice for the employees, the people. They were there to ensure that the organization did care, did value their people, and a skilled HR Practitioner will do just that. They are able to partner and strategize with all levels of business operations to show that the people are valuable.

Now the industry has drastically changed. In fact, right now there is an influx of trendy hip organizations attempting to reinvent HR – ensuring that an HR presence within their organization is truly people-centric. This was the intention and purpose of HR all along, though it is sad to see so many practitioners who have not embraced their purpose. As a result, the industry meets constant resistance and questioning in regard to its value. (But that is a book for another time.)

Despite these dots being connected for me in that moment, this was not when I decided to give in and pursue a career in Human Resources. In fact, if anything the realization made me a bit disgusted for the first time at how some major organizations function. After seeing it happen in that break room, I began to notice it other places as well. I would see it on the faces of employees at retailers, the post office, restaurants and even the doctor's office.

It was hard to witness so much sadness and overall dissatisfaction, especially at my current employer, the large amount of negativity and the miniscule amount of hope that things would ever change or be any better. I refused to allow that to become my life so early on. Regardless, my sort-of-mandated career shift had already left me in a pessimistic state.

I began eating my lunch off-site to avoid the break room, which seemed to be the hub for contagious toxic thoughts. After alternating at a half dozen fast food joints within a 5-mile radius, I found myself drawn routinely back to one restaurant. It was contagious and infectious but in a much different manner.

At this restaurant, the entire staff was simply happy. During the hectic chaotic lunch rush, they still appeared to genuinely enjoy their jobs, and the space felt lighter and more welcoming because of it. The manager led by example, showing true satisfaction in being able to service every customer. I would sit in there for my hour lunch break and just watch in mild admiration, because they were proof – evidence that things could be better. I wasn't quite sure then what the formula was to instill change, or to simply make things better, but I did know it was possible.

BACK AT SCHOOL

I was taking as many courses as possible. Between work and school, I pretty much had no life. Honestly, I wasn't sure why I was paying for an apartment, except to have some place to sleep and store my stuff. The courses I took were dictated by the degree requirements list. When given an option, I chose the course that appeared to demand the least amount of effort. As you can tell, my collegiate pursuit had turned anti-passionate. It was more about the paper, and the degree, to have something to show after all that time and money invested.

The next course on my list at that time was Human Resource Management, which was supposed to give an overview and general foundation to business majors on the world of HR. I quickly classified the course as super easy, requiring pretty much no effort. I found myself connecting with the content like it was common sense to me. As the semester progressed, my ideal academic behaviors began to slack, and even more so for this class. I knew I could easily get B's without doing any reading or even paying attention in class. To be honest, I was struggling with some of my other business-related classes so I consciously, or maybe subconsciously, made the decision to avert all my effort to understanding microeconomics and the theories of supply and demand.

It was in this class that HR chose me – more specifically the professor chose me. We spoke one day after class and Dr. Mary Meisenhelter shared with me that I seemed to be a natural when it came to the HR-related topics. She asked if I had ever considered a career in HR. I chuckled and as respectfully as I could, I let her know I thought it was just an easy class that I had to take for my degree. She ensured me that the class was not easy and that several of my peers were not having as much success.

For the first time in maybe ever, I felt like I was meant to do something – that perhaps this was my sign from the universe that it was what I was meant to do. Between my break room epiphany and this conversation, it couldn't be more blatant.

So I went running into the world of HR, not really ever looking back. I was in a full-on sprint with the intention of no one being able to stop me this time. Unlike music, I knew I could do this. Not only could I do this, but I had the potential to be great at this.

At work, I quickly swapped tracks from retail management to HR Manager. My store supervisor was saddened by the news, and I could tell by his face that he could not comprehend why anyone would willingly want to go into HR. I had just completed the company's Department Manager Training program and we had talked several times before about departments I would be interested in managing. Despite his lack of understanding though, he was supportive and helped me to secure a spot in the company's HR Management Training Program.

I completed that program the summer after my college graduation. In addition, I was given the opportunity to serve as the store's HR Coordinator with the current HR Manager, which counted as an internship and more importantly gave me an idea of what it would be like to work in the field. The HR Manager announced her pregnancy during this time, which allowed me to be exposed even more, assisting her and the store. After she had the baby, I was even allowed to serve as semi-interim-HR-manager on days when the covering HR Manager (who was managing two stores) was unable to be on-site. I asked to move into HR and I was given opportunity after opportunity after opportunity.

The fall following graduation, I was presented the opportunity to be HR Manager of my very own store. It was 2 hours away in a District where I knew pretty much no one. Taking a leap of faith – or maybe a pure drive to not fail again – I said yes. I told myself it was only a temporary gig, the store had lots of "opportunities," and once I helped get them back on track, I could move to a store closer to home.

When I got there, I was overwhelmed by the amount of work needed. From a standpoint of compliance, new hire paperwork and personnel files were practically non-existent. There were several positions open for hire and we were rapidly approaching a busy seasonal period where most stores would double the size of their staff. Policies were not being enforced, particularly the attendance policy. So even though technically we had enough employees, they were not reporting for work and there was a consistent lack of coverage.

In order to maximize my effectiveness, I decided to take a very black and white approach. I did not tolerate excuses and depended heavily on facts in every scenario to hold people accountable. You might say I mastered the progressive disciplinary process to help establish expectations... or to help individuals move on. But to most, I lacked the human element on the outside and did not tolerate behaviors that were counterproductive to the store's goals.

There once was even a rumor that circulated the store that I mentally painted a pink "X" on the backs of my next targets. I always appreciated the nice feminine touch. Despite what people thought of me though, I honestly thought I was doing what was best for the store and the employees.

Inside, there were days I would leave work feeling like a horrible person. On the days that I didn't, I assumed that doing the work I was doing at least made me "not a good person."

Regardless of the employee behavior – if the individual stole, smoked in the store, or just couldn't get to work on time – when you terminate someone you are terminating a piece (or perhaps all) of their livelihood. No matter what the circumstances were, I could never truly associate "good" with what I did day in and day out.

THE TREND

I attempted to adopt a mantra which I still use today when engaging in traditional HR practices of accountability...

You are not doing it to them. They did it to themselves.

When accountability is tackled using a process successfully, it is structured in a fashion so you know that they did it to themselves. In fact, in the process you as an employer will have tried everything that reasonably makes sense to retain that employee.

Today, I coach leaders to ensure the process is done within these guidelines, so it becomes easy to embrace the mantra. However, when I first attempted to adopt the philosophy, I didn't believe it. I still believed deep down inside that I was doing it to them. I believed I was ruining lives... and as punishment I started a self-sabotaging behavior to ruin my own.

I ate. I ate fast food. I ate fast food that was super-sized, or I increased the portions with additional orders. I ate any sort of junk food you could think of in large quantities – whole cakes, packages of cookies, large bags of chips, entire boxes of crackers, and yes... even king-sized Snickers bars or any king-sized candy for that matter.

The high demands of the store meant long hours and minimal time for exercise. When I did have the time to work out, I instead partook in the practice of shopping, which only fed my shopaholic addiction, one I am still recovering from today.

The years that followed continued with this progression, regardless of my position or company. I continued to not heal how I identified myself within, while outside I got bigger and bigger. I went from 185 pounds to 195 pounds, then 200, 205, 210 and 212 when I got married. On my wedding day, my gown was a long flowing white halter-style dress. I picked it because it was the most flattering on my new curvaceous figure. At the time, I felt I looked "the best I could" walking down the aisle, but "beautiful" would not have been a term I would select.

Professionally I was embracing my persona, as lacking a human element with a sense of pride. I began to accept my fate as less "beauty" and more "beast."

A Transformation as Old as Time

The infamous tale of *Beauty and the Beast* is a story of transformation. The curse of the Beast is broken when he is able to change himself. While on the big screen we see the sparkly transformation brought to life by a witch; her true challenge to the Prince was to look within – a curse of personal reflection.

After reading *The Slight Edge*, I now believe time was exposing me during these years, and the path of exposure was the equivalent to a path of self-destruction. I saw myself playing on the edge of a downward spiral, but perhaps exposing the Beast is what it took. Perhaps I needed to show myself such an ugly reflection in order to give myself an ounce of perspective on what was actually happening around me, to challenge myself to start looking within.

Perhaps what I am about to share will sound like a curse upon first read, but have no doubt, it was the curse that transformed me to a place where happily-ever-after is not a myth... it is my everyday way of life.

This journey of transformation was comprised of five major shifts that manifested in different ways. It was the combination of all five which truly awakened within me a person that I had long forgotten.

The shift that I want to share with you first, is one I initially believed was the universe's version of a practical joke.

EXPOSED IN THIS CHAPTER:

1. Determination sometimes arises as the driving force, because we are afraid that our self-worth is being called into question.
2. Refusing to look inward will only cause the outward to get uglier.
3. This book contains the five major shifts to awaken a person you may have long forgotten.

CHAPTER 3

A Sign from the Universe

When I was growing up, my family called it the "cry of the Banshee," like the movie, I suppose. All that I remember though, is that I couldn't control it. And I hated that fact. The lack of control made me feel like such a loser, a weakling. I cried about everything, literally everything. It was also routinely at a level that could be defined as *making a scene*.

A Sea of Strangers

One memory in particular is vividly clear in my mind, perhaps because it still haunts me with embarrassment. It was a family trip to the mall with my mother and brother. I have no idea how old I was at the time, but I must have gotten distracted because I lost them. I found myself alone in a large department store surrounded by endless racks of clothes. As the realization of being lost sank in, the anxiety and fear began to build within me, and the release happened as loud terrible sobs. Sobs so incomprehensible that my words were mere gibberish. Sobs so strong that I had to gasp for air.

This was the cry of the Banshee my family had grown to know and dread.

Quickly a circle of people formed around me, a sea of strangers, but none of them were my mother or brother. Some attempted to take a step closer to comfort me or possibly assist, but their attempts only evoked a louder sob accompanied by a shriek. This ensured that they kept their distance, however they were all still enthralled by the spectacle, staring from all angles.

An event like this would be embarrassing for any mother, but mine had to deal with it on a regular basis.

It was then, between sobs while I tried to attempt to breathe, when I heard my mother's voice. "Sammi," she said quietly and waved her hand above the crowd. I slowly began to move in the direction of her call and the crowd parted to allow me through. My mother didn't say another word. She simply turned and started to walk away with me following behind.

This experience was one of many for me, which created a very clear story. *Tears are a sign of weakness.* In fact, I spent a large amount of my childhood attempting to control this reaction that had earned me the label of "sensitive." By the time I hit high school, the cry of the Banshee had disappeared, but the tear reaction was still inevitable in certain circumstances.

THE FIRST DAY IN PA

When I was 15 years old, my father found his dream job in the city of York, Pennsylvania. So in the summer before my sophomore year of high school my family moved from sunny California to a new place where I knew no one.

I started high school that Fall with a positive attitude and was even optimistic about how it would go. It wasn't until I was sitting in homeroom surrounded by people reuniting after a summer break, that it hit me. The magnitude of the move, the idea that my childhood relationships and friendships would be forever changed or possibly even over completely... that build-up of anxiety and fear started inside, and the release was quiet but the tears were very real. The room grew silent as conversations stopped and the attention focused on me. The strange new girl was crying in the center of the room. There I was surrounded by a sea of strangers again.

The teacher awkwardly avoided the situation entirely, not really knowing how to address an emotional teenager. She spoke to me as if the tears and sniffles weren't happening. In fact, no one around me really knew what to do. I was left alone to console myself until the bell rang for first period. The scene was nowhere as dramatic as the mall incident, however it was enough to establish my identity as the "sensitive girl from California," an identity I had hoped to leave behind.

I began to internalize these experiences as anger, at myself. Every tearful reaction, I viewed as failure.

Future milestones, such as college, jobs, and even dating, became challenges to not reveal my sensitive side. Years and years of this mentality enabled me to build an exterior surface wall that not many could penetrate, and when they did I would crumble only in solitude, bringing my tearful scenes down to almost zero.

The flip side of mastering how to conceal my sensitivity was that when it was exposed, my scenes seemed to be more dramatic than ever – like a movie playing out a great tragedy – an interaction not only emotionally exhausting for myself but for all parties involved. This did no favors for my ability to build strong relationships, which meant that after leaving California friends behind, there was about zero chance of establishing them in Pennsylvania.

An Uncanny Connection

Now I know the picture I am painting is pretty pathetic, but before you assume that I spent my days in Pennsylvania all alone, that was far from the truth. I made "friends" which were more like acquaintances, but I did socialize on some level.

To fill my days, I took a job as a cashier at a local grocery store. It was there that I met Michael. A fellow cashier, with goofy mannerisms and characteristics all around, he shuffled his feet when he walked and said "What?" a lot when he talked. It was the goofiness that made him so entertaining, and for someone not looking for much more than new ways to kill time, he was a perfect match.

Michael and I would banter between our registers and occasionally even chat during our breaks. This eventually grew to seeing each other outside of work, which then somehow evolved to spending almost every day together. For the first time since the move, I found someone that I considered a friend. We referred to each other playfully as "buddies." I had forgotten how nice it was to have someone to talk to, to turn to, to trust.

On top of that, Michael and I had an uncanny connection. I would simply think of him and my phone would buzz with a text. In the middle of conversations, we would finish the other's thought. It was the kind of stuff you read about in romance novels or see in movies. This connection made me begin to question and analyze the relationship. *Was it meant to be something more? Was this what it felt like when you met the one?*

I began to play with the scenario in my mind. *What would it be like to be with Michael in a romantic way? Would the connection be as strong or would it just be weird?* With the constant questioning and imagining, inevitably the word vomit occurred. I told him everything I had been thinking and feeling (or thought I felt), and he sat there and listened. When he attempted to say a word in reply, I stopped him and said, "Forget about it – the whole thing is stupid. Please can we just act like I never said anything?" He told me "sure," and he held up his agreement. Days went on and our friendship actually did continue like the word vomit never happened.

What occurred next is probably the one moment I play routinely in my mind and contemplate whether it's a regret. Instead of allowing our friendship to continue, I resurrected the word vomit. I found myself needing to know his response.

However, at this point in my life, bravery and courage was not a strength. Fearfully I texted, asking if he remembered that day... that day I said I felt more for him... and I asked if he felt the same.

He said "yes," and our relationship was transformed almost immediately from best buddies to newly dating, a level of relationship I was not ready for. At the time, I could barely believe that someone would want to be my friend. How could I have ever thought I would be able to believe that someone would want to be more?

The next month or two was all a blur, a blur of drama. I'll give Michael credit, he tried. He tried to hold on, but we were too young and it was too much. Perhaps I was too much for anyone. My constant need for reassurance had to be exhausting, so it wasn't surprising when Michael slowly began to pull away. The text messages, phone calls, and visits dwindled from daily to every other day, to once a weekend, to sometimes no response at all, until finally during one of my text pleas for reassurance a simple reply came: "I can't do this anymore." And just like that, it was over. Everything gone, not just boyfriend but best friend.

Saying I was devastated would be putting it lightly. Acquaintances tried to comfort and console me as I grieved this monumental loss. I retreated and began to build my protective walls again. That wasn't the last I heard of Michael, though. A few weeks later he called to see how I was doing. I could hear in the tone of his voice the concern and almost reassurance that he still cared.

Michael stirred something within me that I hadn't felt in a long time. He exposed a side of me that I had been desperately trying to hide from the world for fear of a lack of acceptance. Yet when he exposed me and walked away, he didn't run... and he certainly didn't hide. I will be forever grateful.

The nature of the loss I experienced from this relationship awoke in me the true cry of the Banshee. For nearly a year, I would cry myself to sleep and periodically break down throughout the day. The cries were ugly, loud, and raw. Michael truly awoke something in me that I had convinced myself I had made disappear.

In truth, I hadn't made it disappear. I had only found ways to numb myself and feel less. If I couldn't feel, it lessened the likelihood of a tearful reaction. But choosing not to feel is choosing to not authentically connect to others. It is choosing to not love others, and in return, losing the right to expect love in return.

SIGNS

Do you believe in signs? Have you ever asked for a sign? Wanted something to give you reassurance that you were on the right path? I know I did time and time again. It seemed that with every misstep I became less trusting of myself and instead seeking some outward sign, looking for a divine message or direction for how I should live my life. I was so afraid and almost desperate to not be wrong that I wished someone else would tell me how to live... because I couldn't be left to lead my own life. Every time I tried, I only screwed it up more. I clearly was not capable of knowing what was best for myself.

My spiritual teacher, Gabrielle Bernstein, often talks about noticing "signs" as ways to get answers from the universe. She references things like owls or colors or numbers as signs, saying that if you see that particular item, it is a sign that you are heading in the right direction, and that someone has your back.

I believe my sign is the cry of the Banshee. My gift is not cute or something I treasure. In fact, it is something I avoid. In its authentic raw form, my cry of the Banshee is ugly. It is the quintessential definition of an ugly cry.

According to Wikipedia, a Banshee is a "female spirit in Irish mythology who heralds the death of a family member, usually by shrieking. She can appear in a variety of forms. Perhaps most often she is seen as an ugly, frightful hag, but she can also appear young and beautiful if she chooses."

The origin of this myth being Irish caught me off guard. Of course, I don't know for sure who first started calling my loud shrieking the cry of the Banshee, but I always assumed it was my mother in cahoots with her sisters, as a joke or game others would find entertaining. However, my mother is of Filipino descent, while my father is German and Irish. Now knowing the origin of this word, it makes me wonder if my father had any involvement.

The power of this sign for me becomes apparent through its definition. The shrieking is made in reaction to death. It is meant to share and express a deep-rooted loss – eerily similar to the awakening my break-up with Michael brought to life.

The other piece of the definition that caught my attention is that the Banshee can appear in a variety of forms, one that is ugly and frightful, and another which is young and beautiful. The difference is in how the Banshee chooses to be seen.

From its initial resurrection, I thought the cry was ugly and frightful to others. In the case of Michael, I believe the Banshee characteristics were what scared him away. Over the years I've finally realized that what I was missing all along is the *beauty* of this cry – since it can only be seen if I choose. I had spent so much time hiding the ugliness, when really that was going to be the key to making me beautiful again. From the inside out.

I'm sure you are wondering what in the world I'm talking about. Let's process the initial unleash of the cry of the Banshee in my semi-adult career. That ugly cry was not cued until Michael – my first love – left. Now as an adult, married with children, I finally know and truly understand what love is. I can look back and see that he was the first. That helps in justifying how badly it hurt when he was gone. The pain that resonated within me caused ugly cry after ugly cry, shrieking sobs as I tried to fall to sleep to calm my mind and heart.

This happened right before high school graduation and I shut off from the world around me, essentially numb when I wasn't sobbing. In the moment I was blind and wanted only to turn back time, or have another opportunity to see Michael again so I could change everything. So I could make all the pain go away. Make him not leave. So I could have him back. Ridiculous, but true.

I am sure many of you have processed a heartache similarly. In that moment, I only could find blame with myself. It was my failure. It was something wrong with me. It was the confirmation I needed that I would always be alone.

But with all that said, you may remember that even after he had gone, he reached out enough to let me know he cared, and that his compassion was real and not from a place of strictly empathy. In that moment, the beauty of being given the opportunity to love and be loved still fills my soul to this day. Michael gave me just that – the beautiful opportunity. No, it wasn't the epic love story of a lifetime. We aren't soulmates waiting to reconnect. But if he hadn't presented that opportunity there is a big chance I might never have seized the opportunity when I did meet "the one."

WHEN WE ARE LOST

When we are lost and signs attempt to present themselves, they are not filled with reassurance and comfort. In fact, they are filled with quite the opposite. They are uncomfortable and loaded with fear.

In *The Slight Edge*, a cue associated with the success curve is doing actions early on that are uncomfortable. When success is reached, then these actions become more comfortable. The signs we all seek for reassurance become comfortable the closer we get to who we are meant to be, what we are meant to do, and how we are supposed to live.

The amount of fear and discomfort associated with a sign that presents itself can serve as a gauge to determine how far we are along our path, and what direction we are heading. I think for most of us, we drastically underestimate fear. We don't fully comprehend how fear paralyzes us, essentially making us stagnant in pursuit of our dreams.

Remember how I was terrified to perform my vocal audition for college admissions? I can see now how my fear paralyzed me – literally – from performing to my full potential. I became so frozen as a result of this fear that I deemed my dream impossible. *I* deemed it impossible... not some greater guiding power... or fate. *Me.*

I don't know about you, but I am a big fan of deflecting. Deflecting as much attention and focus away from myself and to others. This practice can also be called neglecting, because ultimately what I am doing when I deflect is neglecting myself. I could easily make the argument that the deflecting was actually an act of service, putting others before myself to serve a calling greater than me. But in truth, it's an excuse because focusing on me is uncomfortable. So naturally I would do anything to avoid it. This was a discomfort I could only avoid for so long before the act of being selfish became a need for emotional survival, which is the next shift I want to share with you.

EXPOSED IN THIS CHAPTER:

1. Choosing not to feel is choosing to not authentically connect to others. It is choosing to not love others, and in return, losing the right to expect love in return.

2. The difference in the perspective, and ultimate lesson, comes from how the Banshee chooses to be seen.

3. When we are lost and signs attempt to present themselves, they are not filled with reassurance and comfort. In fact, they are filled with quite the opposite. They are uncomfortable and loaded with fear.

4. The signs we all seek for reassurance become comfortable the closer we get to who we are meant to be, what we are meant to do, and how we are supposed to live.

5. Ultimately when I deflect, I am neglecting myself.

CHAPTER 4

THE SELFISH NECESSITY

In college, just like every great love, my boyfriend (who later became my husband) and I split for reasons that still aren't 100% clear today. The one thing he can articulate to me about that time is that he knows he felt like he needed a break. Not to see other people or even to experience anything in particular, but to simply be on his own. If it isn't obvious yet, he was the one who made the decision for the break, and I didn't really have a say. I was left to deal with the unknown destiny of our relationship. Maybe he would come back but there was an equal chance he would not.

If this truly was the end of our relationship, I had to decide if I was going to wait around, or start healing. Let's be honest, initially I waited. For weeks and potentially months, my life pretty much stopped and those who chose to keep me company had to deal with (on the best days) solemn Samm and (on the bad days) super sad sobbing Samm.

I could see in the eyes of those who tried to be there for me, that they were completely lost as to what to even attempt to do. In addition, the heaviness of feelings didn't lighten as time went on. This began to concern me as well. After about a week of walking by the Campus Counseling Center, I finally went in and made an appointment. I felt pathetic, needing a counselor for a boy. But I was even more surprised when those sessions quickly shifted from conversations about heartache to the loneliness to my childhood.

Now here's my disclaimer: relationships within family, romance and friendships, all involve two people. In some cases, two very different people. I believe we make an assumption when it comes to family, and particularly our children, that it's not possible for them to be much different from us. I believe logically we think that because we made them, they are literally part of us. We develop an instant blind eye to the individuality and uniqueness we have brought into the world. In fact, there are whole books now on coaching and advising the next generation of parents to respect that individuality and allow it to flourish as the child grows. This feels counterintuitive. I mean you're the parent, right? We should naturally know what's best for our children. However, I remember not too long ago being terrified when expecting my first child, thinking I had no clue what I was doing.

I say all this because I was fortunate to have two very loving parents who provided me with an amazing life. The thing is, I looked and sounded like my mother... but on the inside I thought and felt like my father. This perfect blend was easily hidden from the world, and as a result it meant that I was pushed based off my mother's limits rather than from the introverted nature I held within – the part of myself that empowered me to feel deeply and analyze unyieldingly. What might be a simple interaction or occurrence for my mother could potentially be devastating and paralyzing to me.

This is something I could never articulate as a child and therefore when I made a statement like, "I'm scared," the magnitude of what I meant was never heard. The absence of this knowledge for my mother specifically resulted in some very interesting formative events for me as a child. Most, I would guess are not even on her radar. Once again, completely not her fault. In fact, it is this entire scenario that terrifies me about being a parent now.

That year in college at the counseling center, I learned an ounce about who I was authentically for the very first time. I was affirmed that my feelings weren't wrong and what I needed out of a relationship was not outlandish either. It was the first time I became able to articulate my true definition of love. Most of my childhood conclusions came to a desire for more hugs, I love you's, and heart-to-hearts. These are things I intentionally try to do with my daughters, however I am completely aware that this list may not meet their own individual definition of what they need to feel loved.

In my career, I have come into contact with several women with a high level of maternal instinct. They loved to give me hugs, have heart-to-hearts, and some even told me they loved me. Regardless of whether they verbally articulated it or not, I felt loved. I welcomed it and almost craved that sort of connection, that I felt had been missing for so long.

When I met April, I knew that she possessed a high level of maternal instinct. Anytime we would be at the same networking event or party she couldn't help it – the instinct would kick in and she would hug me and listen intently to me out of love. She even watched my non-verbal cues, so a simple "I'm fine" would not suffice in escaping her embrace. If you were not 100% she would know, and she wanted to know why and she wanted to genuinely help. I cannot think of a conversation where before it was over she didn't say, "Please let me know if there is anything I can do, I'm here." And it was always nice to hear. It's nice to have people like that around you.

Therefore, when an opportunity presented itself for April to possibly work and assist me professionally, I seized it. I know deep down that the invitation was mostly selfish. I wanted her maternal instinct around more. I wanted to guarantee that every single day I would feel loved and I knew that she would deliver.

What makes April so beautiful is that she loves so much. She gives most of her time to helping others. She drives people around to their appointments, cleans their homes, and is always accessible for a good heart-to-heart when needed. As such an active person, I felt it would be obvious that April could sustain solid performance. Instead it was more of a roller coaster.

The highs of working together made me hopeful this could have a happy ending. But the lows were only bearable for so long, because I valued the highs so much. Over time, the highs and lows no longer seemed so different, and when April's performance started to level out, it was like she wasn't there at all.

This made me furious and once again I took it to a selfish place. She had awoken the cry of the Banshee, only this time it was more of a screech, a terrible scream. I screamed, "How could you do this to me and take advantage of this fantastic opportunity I provided you?" But as we have already learned, this screech comes from a place that's honoring a loss. I already knew that losing her was inevitable.

It shouldn't be a surprise that her resignation followed shortly, and was necessary if we wanted to save whatever relationship we had left. In that conversation, the Banshee returned again, this time in the form of the ugly cry, where I shared my love and gratitude for her.

I had hired April in an attempt to fulfill my own selfish needs. I didn't meet her in the middle. Instead I dragged her across and almost trapped her. I was an ugly person to someone who cared for me so much. Sometimes I wonder what would've happened if I had instead met her in the middle. Perhaps we'd still be working together, or maybe our friendship would have grown deeper. Regardless, I am grateful for the lesson.

While choosing not to put yourself last, you must also be wary of acting from a place of selfish goals, as I had with April. Meeting in the middle is the only way to have a truly healthy relationship for both parties involved. It is when both individuals have their selfish needs met.

THE LESSON

The lesson is short and simple, but powerful. My needs are essential to my success. If I choose to put myself last, I am choosing to send a message to the universe that says I don't want to be successful. This applies in all areas of life and I am telling you if you are not having success in one area of your life, it is because you are neglecting yourself.

This applies to your marriage, friendships, family relationships, and yes, even work relationships. The next story is a perfect example of how I completely disregarded my selfish needs and as a result almost ended my career.

MY WANNABE MINI-ME

Raquel first appeared in my life as a trainee. I had her for new employee orientation and a few required trainings. Raquel made it known how much she enjoyed my facilitation style and that she hoped she could do it one day as well.

Now that she had been brought to my attention, I watched and observed her in a different way. In some ways I began to mentor before being asked.

Primarily I was looking for the essentials – whether she exhibited traits to become a facilitator and trainer. She was a natural, so I wanted to reach out and help in any way I could.

Becoming a trainer was not a position that was handed to me. I had to work my butt off. I had to prove myself. I had to go back to school and get a Master's degree, so I could have a piece of paper that would tell the world, "Yes, I know what I am doing." I would have given anything for someone to take an interest in me and mentor me. So I decided if that was what Raquel wanted, I would do anything within my control to help.

Eventually the relationship was formalized and Raquel began reporting to me. I wanted so badly to not screw it up. I introduced her to my fellow colleagues and asked for their input. They all seemed to see what I saw – loads of potential and much success in her future.

Potential wasn't the only thing that kept me tied to Raquel. As I began to learn about her, I realized she reminded me of myself, which made my connection to her stronger. It's safe to say I put my career on hold for about eight months as I dedicated my time and effort to making her successful.

That included everything from work-life balance to rate of pay. Money is a topic I rarely like to approach. In fact, in my early employment days, when the first payday rolled around, I checked my bank account but no money had been deposited. I actually almost convinced myself not to approach my employer, thinking I had the dates screwed up and the money would show up eventually.

Yes, I hated talking about money so much that I would actually consider working without pay, rather than talking about it and getting it resolved.

But for Raquel, I talked about money in great lengths. How could I give her more? If she needed money to feel secure, I felt compelled to get that resolved so this obstacle could be removed and not hold her back from her own success.

As time progressed, I kept throwing opportunities Raquel's way even when she was falling flat. I couldn't understand the disconnect by the bright star I saw in front of me, yet who couldn't deliver in front of others. We had several heart-to-hearts where I was honest yet affirming that this was hers for the taking.

Eventually, I could no longer justify her compensation. Raquel was not performing and there was no indication that it was going to change. And instead of her showing signs of understanding, she insisted on more money, saying that she was worth more. When I was honest (with myself and her) and told her that I couldn't justify a recommendation to leadership for a salary increase, she started looking for employment elsewhere.

Soon she found employment full-time, at a place that wasn't her dream, but the compensation was what she needed. She offered to stay with us on a part-time basis, stating that this was her dream and she hoped that one day she could do it full-time. I was in shock to hear that she had taken full-time employment elsewhere without discussing it with me first. As expected, we scheduled a time to meet and talk about the transition of some of her full-time duties and to discuss what part-time would look like, including any necessary changes to her compensation.

It was during this conversation that something within me stirred. A part of me couldn't fathom how someone who was presented the opportunity to pursue their dream could so easily walk away... how someone I had put so much faith and trust in, could just give up. Perhaps it was the reality check of where I stood in her world of priorities and how harshly that contrasted with where she stood in mine. In the middle of a perfectly logical, professional conversation, the cry of the Banshee was unleashed in response to the upcoming great loss that was about to occur. The loss of a great talent, fellow dreamer, and friend.

As I engaged in this ugly cry, I shared with Raquel everything that I had seen in her and that I only wanted her to be happy. If this decision was what was required, then I supported it wholeheartedly. But I wanted to make sure she knew what I saw within her. I wanted to make sure this decision would not be regretted in the future. And I hoped she could feel how much I cared for and valued our relationship. Raquel cried too as we exchanged words, so I took that as a sign that we were on the same vibration, or at least the same page... that the words I said were delivered just as they should.

Raquel transitioned to part-time and I went from seeing her every day to once a week, to basically not at all. After 30 days, I received an email from her asking yet again for an increase in compensation. She stated that she was worth more and her pay was making the part-time work not worth her time.

In that month, Raquel's performance hadn't changed at all, so therefore I couldn't justify a recommendation for an increase. After she learned that an increase was not in the cards, she submitted her letter of resignation, with less than one week's notice. In addition, she stated I had created a work environment which made it impossible for her to stay. This final statement convinced HR that it was best for me not to handle her resignation and instead limit speaking to her altogether.

I saw Raquel once more, on her last day when she gave me an update on a transitioning project. I kept my mouth shut, knowing my words before must've been damaging rather than full of love as I had intended.

After nearly a year of me giving and her taking, I was left with nothing but cleaning up and starting over.

IT WAS EXTREME BUT NECESSARY

It was amazing to learn in retrospect how many people around me noticed Raquel draining me, but said nothing. When I inquired why, they all replied that I wouldn't have listened.

We all welcome loud distractions, but this one left me completely blind. Looking back, the one message that rings clear is that I had written myself off. When I took Raquel under my wing, I told the universe to forget about me. "There is no hope for me, it's too late, invest in someone else." I essentially said I didn't matter.

My selfish need to know that I was worthy of happiness, success, and hope... my selfish need to know that I mattered... my selfish need to know that "I am enough, just as I am..." was ignored completely. I was so caught up in the attempt to meet Raquel's needs, that I completely ignored my own.

This resulted in a lot of backwards steps for me, both personally and professionally. It was reckless and left me in a place where I had to actively seek out help to restore what was once me.

The relationship with Raquel had been extremely one-sided, making it impossible to sustain. Relationships and support are essential to well-being. It is human nature to desire connection. However, we must make sure these relationships are healthy, otherwise they could do more damage than good.

There is one major attribute that is present in every healthy relationship: it is that the two parties are able to meet in the middle. Call it compromise, empathy, or just being fair. I call it the next shift worthy to be shared.

EXPOSED IN THIS CHAPTER:

1. We can develop an instant blind eye to the individuality and uniqueness in this world.
2. If you are not having success in one area of your life, it is because you are neglecting yourself.
3. Meeting in the middle is the only way to have a truly healthy relationship.
4. Ignoring your own needs is the equivalent of taking steps backwards personally and professionally.
5. Unhealthy relationships have the power to do more damage than good.

CHAPTER 5

MEET ME IN THE MIDDLE

If there is one thing I have learned about relationships, it is that it truly takes two people to tango. A successful relationship, romantic or otherwise, cannot be sustained unless both parties are willing to come to the table. Showing up is not enough. They have to see the bigger picture of the relationship and know exactly why that connection is so valuable.

The significance of the relationship is key, because they must become willing to be open – open to realize that they are not innocent, and also that they are not the victim. We all have something we can own. Whether it is because we made the initial action that caused conflict, or because we were the one who stubbornly prevented the healing process from initiating.

The biggest transformation I have seen in myself as I have grown is in understanding relationships for what they really are. Before, relationships were more of a social objective or culture goal, to have so many friends or be romantically involved. However, the real significance is to provide support and balance when we need it. These are essential in empowering us to reach our end-goals and ultimate purpose. When we decide to neglect a relationship and not meet someone in the middle, we essentially stall our path. We create obstacles and make things harder for ourselves. We pretty much create the fate we were so fearfully trying to avoid.

But before we can reap the benefits that these smarter relationships can provide us, we must remember that *both* individuals need to meet in the middle. While we must neither under- or over-extend ourselves, we must also make sure the other individual is responsible for their half of the contribution.

And finally, but most importantly, we must know what it means for us when someone consciously decides *not* to meet us in the middle.

THE HARD LESSON OF MARRIAGE

After a dozen years together and five years of marriage, if there is one thing my husband and I have learned, it's that compromise is essential. When you make the decision to be with another person, if you are unable to move your ego aside occasionally, you will be unable to develop a relationship that provides mutual fulfillment. In that instance, someone would always get the short end of the stick... and if you are the one refusing to let go of your ego, guess what – the person you claim to love more than anything else in the world, will be getting the short end of the stick *because of you.*

It took me and my husband a decade to understand the significance that compromise plays in a relationship, and the only reason we learned that lesson is because we were both ready to come to a place somewhere in the middle.

In September of 2015, my marriage had become distant. I was engaging in a constant blame game towards my husband for my unhappiness. Then on Labor Day it imploded. After we arrived home from a Family Picnic, he approached me in our home office and told me we needed to talk. In a matter of minutes, whatever safety and security I had from our relationship disappeared. The only thing I felt certain about in my life, was no more. Even though he hadn't said it was over, he made it pretty clear that he wasn't sure anything could change it.

I was completely unable to process what I was hearing. So I did the only thing I could do at the time... I ran away.

I needed to get out and away, where hopefully I could breathe again. For the first time since moving to Pennsylvania, I called a friend out of pure necessity. My world was crashing and I was falling fast. I needed someone to reach out and grab me.

My friend MaryRose answered the phone and heard only my uncontrollable sobs and the words, "Can I come over?" When I arrived there, I fell to pieces on the couch in front of her and her husband. Recapping the entire conversation and trying to make sense of how something could change so quickly, I heard my phone occasionally buzz with text messages and phone calls. All were from my husband Josh, trying to check in and see if I was okay. He had no idea where I had gone, but he'd seen the state I was in when I left – definitely not a state that anyone should be driving in.

After what seemed like a marathon of sobbing and talking in circles, I could finally breathe again. I had exhausted my emotions and the fog began to lift enough for me to ask, "What's next?"

I asked MaryRose and her husband, Chad, "What do I do? Do I go home? Do I get the kids? Do I go to my parents?"

Chad who had been listening intently as I poured my soul out, was the first to answer. "Whoa whoa," he cautioned. "Who said anything about your marriage being over? I know Josh loves you, so before you start planning what's next, you are going to call him and tell him that you're okay – because he is probably worried sick about you. Then you are going to go home and the two of you are going to continue talking. This isn't over until you both decide that it is."

I couldn't argue with his logic. I did exactly that and called my husband, affirming to him that I was okay, and then I went home to start a conversation that inched us closer to the middle.

MAKE ME READY

The fact that I am still married today as I write this means the conversation was successful. In fact, as a result, our relationship is more fulfilling than ever, for both of us.

But one fact became evident as we journeyed through this extremely challenging, heart-wrenching time. If this had happened five years earlier, he and I both know I wouldn't have come back home. There would have been no way I could've started that conversation. My marriage would have ended... the most significant relationship of my life... would have been over... just like that.

So what changed? What made me ready to come meet him in the middle? I certainly knew I needed him. I knew that he provided balance and support that I absolutely needed in my life, but that alone was not enough to make me ready.

THE ART OF PEOPLE PLEASING

If you are anything like me, you're a people pleaser.

People pleasers enter relationships with an uncanny ability to put their own thoughts, feelings, wants, and needs on a shelf. They focus all their energies on the thoughts, feelings, wants, and needs of the other, desiring nothing more than to feel like they have substantially contributed – which is disturbingly not unlike trying to control someone else's happiness.

The wonderful world of Hollywood uses drama to create thrilling films. But life is not a movie. When drama occurs in real life, we must wake up the following day and handle the consequences.

What most of us are seeking is peace – an internal peace and harmony within ourselves, knowing that we have exactly what we need, and are where we need to be in any given moment.

Our culture, however, paints the picture of "wants," driving us to purchase material goods to secure our peace. But happiness cannot be found in a store, and it certainly cannot be bought. It lives within us waiting for the day that we will be open to listening.

I entered my marriage just like any other relationship. The fear of being alone was so terrifying that I would rather have companionship of any sort than face the alternative. My main goal was simply to make sure he didn't leave. I strived to become what my husband wanted and needed, hiding any thoughts and feelings of my own which might jeopardize the status quo.

Marriage is a funny thing. The dynamics from boyfriend to fiancé to husband change drastically. Your personal space becomes less, especially once you share a bed. Inside, I finally recognized on some level the appeal of being married but having separate twin beds side by side. I also, quickly understood the trends of man-caves and she-sheds. When personal space becomes a premium, it becomes easy to forget who we are and where the marriage begins. More importantly, we forget who we were before the relationship.

After saying "I do," some days I felt as if I were living a lie, trying so hard to be this impossible creature of perfection... trying so hard to cleanse myself of behaviors that contradicted the "perfect wife" image. The facade only got heavier as time passed.

By the time we reached the breaking point, I was so tired. I was tired of pretending that our marriage was perfect and that my husband was everything that I needed. I soon realized that the entire thing had been a facade for him as well.

I've since come to the conclusion that you cannot fake relationships. Marriage is the ultimate vulnerable relationship that we enter into and promise to give of ourselves in a way we promise to no other.

When my marriage was on the rocks, I was given a gift – the opportunity to reevaluate what I wanted and needed from this relationship. My husband had wanted the same chance, so we began to meet regularly with a therapist who could help guide us through the process. I quickly found myself using those sessions selfishly, pushing the envelope by putting out whatever raw but authentic emotion or voice arose. I no longer sat back and listened to what my husband wanted and needed, trying to change myself so I could become that.

The beauty of one's marriage almost ending is that once you have a taste of the pain and heartache, it completely changes the circumstances under which you will enter into that relationship again. Perhaps it was the necessary step needed for me to have any chance at a healthy marriage. A happy marriage.

During this time of healing, regardless of how painful and uncertain it was, we equally felt a weight or barrier had been lifted, allowing us to be more intimate than ever. I hope by now you have learned that the true intimate connection we all crave is beyond the bedroom, on a level that resonates with your core. It's your soul being exposed and being accepted.

For almost a year, my cry of the Banshee came unyieldingly into my home. Sometimes it was every night and even though I felt like the ugly cry caused me to mumble nonsense and gibberish, I felt the most authentic I had ever been in my marriage. The triggers for this ugly cry would spark exhausting but necessary discussion between the two of us, and for the first time in nearly ten years we talked about all the things which had been left unsaid.

Not a day goes by now that I take my marriage for granted. This entire experience ingrained in me how much hard work a satisfying relationship is. Therefore, I live each day as if my husband might not be here tomorrow. When you embrace this shift, it puts things into perspective and makes it possible to never go to bed angry at one another, to kiss often, and to find time for just the two of you to cherish. It makes all that cheesy but so-true marriage advice sound reasonable and valuable.

OWN WHAT YOU CAN OWN

Author Gabrielle Bernstein often suggests: "Clean up your side of the street." This concept points out that before we can engage in the blame game or pass judgment on another, we must first take care of what we need to own.

Let's initially think about this from a literal sense. Think of a neighbor whose house is across the street. Every morning you come out of your home and shake your head as you look over at your neighbor's house. Their yard is full of weeds and they clearly have not mowed in weeks. The paint is peeling, there are dead plants throughout the garden, and the trash is overflowing into the street – and it's not even trash day.

This neighbor is prime for picking when it comes to neighborhood gossip, but before you should say one judgmental word, you need to turn around and look at your own house. Is it perfect? Is it pristine? Perhaps parts of it, but perfection is a myth. There is always something that can be better. That goes the same for us as individuals. Life is a journey, not a destination.

This next example is equally as simple in nature, but it's a true story that illustrates the point. I went through a period of time in my career where I frequently found myself in the following predicament. I held a job with a challenging supervisor (challenging in a non-motivating, completely unhealthy way). The circumstances reached a point where I made the decision to leave my position without having first secured a new job.

One reason for this was that I was so traumatized by this constant pattern happening in my career, that I continually second guessed myself in the job search process. I did not trust myself to select an organization and position to apply for, out of fear that I would just replay the next round of the pattern again. I became highly selective and did many many Google searches on the organizations before ever submitting my resume.

This is when I found the one job where I actually knew the supervisor. Tracey Aust had been an adjunct professor at my college. She was the one who introduced me to the world of Corporate Training & Development and inspired me to shift my career from a focus in Employee Relations to Training. The idea of being able to work and possibly be mentored by the same person who'd inspired me, sounded like perfection. The only issue was that it was a Training job and they were looking for someone with relevant experience – and my background was a bit of a stretch. To top it off, it was a position in healthcare, while my background then was 10 years in retail. Despite knowing nothing about healthcare, I applied and surprisingly got a call back.

After five months of interviews, I was made an offer and started my career in the healthcare industry. Tracey and I began building our relationship and figuring out the dynamics of working together. As expected, we hit our first little bump in the road, the test of conflict that either strengthens or weakens an infant relationship.

My work shift was from about 8:30 in the morning to between 4 and 4:30 in the afternoon. As a new employee, my daily schedule consisted of morning training or shadowing Tracey, and then ended in my own cubicle, working on various projects. At the end of the day as I would pack up to leave, I would see the light on in Tracey's office. I questioned whether or not I should stop in and say "bye" before heading out.

Now, let's put some more context around why I would ponder this question. I am extremely introverted at my core, so my first instinct is to over-observe and over-analyze everything. One of my past supervisors was not a fan of end-of-day farewells, viewing them as interruptions. This perspective had definitely stayed with me.

As a new employee, I desperately wanted to leave a perfect first impression. As a result of these prior circumstances, I decided to not say goodbye. I cleaned up for the day, logged off my computer, and headed out.

The next morning, I greeted Tracey in her office and got comfortable to learn what was on that day's agenda. "Samm, before we get started," she said, "there is something I would like to talk to you about." I took a big gulp and nodded for her to continue. My mind was already racing to what I might have done or forgotten to do. Tracey went on to inquire why I hadn't said goodbye at the end of the day. Then she shared all the stories she had made up in her head, which varied from me hating my job to me simply slacking off and cutting out early.

I sighed relief and apologized, sharing my goodbye dilemma. Honestly, I couldn't believe we were having a conversation about such a menial action. However, it was a perfect display of how menial actions have the power to derail relationships. If Tracey had not initiated the conversation with me to clear the air, the stories her mind created would have impacted our working relationship, and possibly haunted my career at that organization. This was the very first time, I witnessed what it takes to meet someone in the middle. That blatant move engraved in me a level of respect for Tracey that I still hold to this day.

In every circumstance, there is something we can own, and indeed that we *must* own, if we have any hope of truly creating a healthy relationship. If we remain in denial and choose to engage in blame, the relationship will deteriorate. The same is true if someone is blaming you, judging you, and owning nothing. The decision is yours to take steps to heal the relationship... or end it.

Our undeniable human desire to connect, despite expected challenges and possible rejection, is actually worth it. The value is found when you discover people who will meet you halfway. Once you establish a foundation of these synced relationships you'll have a firm ground to stand on for the next shift I would like to share – being able to see the doors of opportunity open to you, once you begin to own what you need to own.

EXPOSED IN THIS CHAPTER:

1. What most of us are seeking is peace – an internal peace and harmony within ourselves.
2. The true intimate connection we all crave is beyond the bedroom, on a level that resonates with your core. It's your soul being exposed and being accepted.
3. Before we can engage in the blame game or pass judgment on another, we must first take care of what we need to own.
4. There will come a test of conflict that will either strengthen or weaken an infant relationship.
5. Menial actions have the power to derail relationships.

CHAPTER 6

Seeing the Door Open

I can't recall the specific event, but I will never forget who was at my table. I was still in a place of feeling trapped in my own misery. My life lacked purpose and I felt like I was just aimlessly wandering, hoping that around some corner I could find a little joy. I was determined to make my current life work because those were the cards I had been dealt as a result of falling completely and utterly in love.

My husband on the other hand had life figured out since high school. He interned with the financial team that he currently works with, and once he decided he was going to be a financial advisor, he never looked back. No obstacle was ever too large for him to overcome, in fact challenges only made him more driven. This success has made it possible for him to be an awesome provider. We have also been invited to all kinds of events where I got the opportunity to meet and interact with incredible leaders of local organizations.

As I look back on my life and try to find a time where I felt something besides numbness, one of my fond memories is from college, when hired as a website designer by the local Health Education Center. I had taught myself to code in high school and never considered pursuing it in college, therefore I had no legitimate training. Talk about feeling unqualified and uncomfortable. I would frequently volunteer to help with other projects around the organization so I could feel like I was actually contributing.

The center hosted several field trips for local schools where they educated children on healthy habits. We got to play with puppets and large toothbrushes. It was awesome. I enjoyed every moment, so much so that when I moved back home to York, PA, and found myself randomly driving by our local Health Education Center, I would begin reminiscing, usually followed by a quick gander on their website to see if they were hiring. Even though it was a completely different center, it still reminded me of a place that had made me so happy.

So at the event I attended with my husband, we wound up seated across from the Director of our local Health Education Center. My husband, being the wonderful man that he is, quickly connected the dots. He not only made the introduction but jumped right in with, "In college, Samm worked at the local Health Education Center and loved it..." leaving things completely open for a conversation to spark and allowing me to share what had brought me so much joy. Before I left that evening, the Director and I exchanged business cards, and she invited me to come in for a tour so she could show me around and chat more.

That was the last time I talked to her. I left that evening feeling a high of hope for what was to come. But I never called, I didn't even email. I just let the card sit there... and the days, weeks, and years passed.

I Thought I Was Ready

Clearly a door had been opened for me, one that I was asking to open for quite a while. I guess if you are persistent enough with the universe, it will finally cave and give in to you. But then it becomes like a slap in the face, when you realize that perhaps what you wanted is not what you are quite ready for at that moment.

This story illustrates the doors of opportunity that most of us are conditioned to see – in the way in which our culture has defined opportunity – however, there are numerous other doors presented to us every day. These doors are not so easily spotted, especially if we are allowing life to whisk away at lightning speed. These doors come in the forms of opportunities to learn, grow, and nurture the skills and abilities that we need to get where we ultimately want to go.

One particular door started to appear for me five years before it completely materialized. While I was pursuing my undergraduate degree, that year that HR chose me, I had transitioned to HR Coordinator for the retail store where I worked. The position was not in the store budget, so to justify it, I was given a blend of collective responsibilities. I was okay with that. All that mattered was that I had enough HR-related responsibilities to be able to count the experience as an internship.

Among my random duties assigned, I was asked to assist in representing the store in a non-profit agency's event. It was an experience that I honestly dreaded but which turned out to not be so bad. I learned a lot about the agency that day and developed a high level of respect for the work they were doing in the community. I did my volunteer time and then moved on. Honestly, I never looked back.

Five years later, I was preparing to launch Leadership Arts Associates and almost frantically seeking advice from anyone who was willing to give it. One of my colleagues suggested that I get involved on some non-profit boards, which sounded pretty painless. As a way of embracing this suggestion and sending vibes of "bring it on," I remember updating my LinkedIn profile to indicate I was interested in volunteer opportunities, and included what types of work I would be most passionate about.

This prompted a friend to make contact and say that he knew a non-profit agency which was looking for board members, and it just so happened to be the same agency I'd worked in partnership with five years earlier. I took this as an easy sign. I knew it was an agency I could get passionate about, so I immediately said, "Yes, how do I get involved?"

It turned out the non-profit agency was going through a large transition, including the loss of their

Executive Director. Securing my volunteer involvement was placed on hold. Months passed, but right about the time I had forgotten the offer, I received an email connecting me with the new Executive Director to set up a time to discuss volunteer leadership roles.

This truly was my first venture into the world of non-profit board service and I had no idea what to expect at this meeting with the Executive Director. Upon arriving that day, I hadn't done much to prepare, assuming the conversation would be pretty chill... more a getting-to-know-you session. I was taken aback when the Director began a formal interview, inquiring about my background and work experience. After she finished with her questions and asked if I had any, she thanked me for my time and began to explain her vision.

She shared how she was seeking passionate people with a strong foundation in their faith to help get this agency back to its origins of doing God's work. She then shared that she had not heard anything similar from me and therefore wasn't certain I would be a good match for what the organization needed at that moment.

I instantly felt judged as not being someone of faith. I could feel the cry of the Banshee begin to swirl within me, as I stumbled over my words to explain how for the last 10 years I had been an HR practitioner where being neutral was a necessity, making no place for my faith to be displayed publicly. However, my faith had always been a guiding force behind all that I had accomplished, and even more so, it was the reason why I created Leadership Arts Associates. Put in its simplest form, I had felt *called*. For the first time ever in my career, I poured out how my faith facilitated my success and how I believed it had brought me to that moment.

The Director looked at me as I tried to compose myself, wiping the messy tears that drenched my entire face. Her demeanor completely changed. In response she shared her story of being guided by faith to this moment. It was like we connected almost instantly. She asked if I would be interested in starting on the Faith Relations Committee with the intention of eventually working towards a position on the Board. She expressed that she felt this would be the best path for me, a place where I could maximize my impact to the agency. I agreed, wholeheartedly trusting her guidance on where I could best help in achieving their mission moving forward. We embraced like close friends when saying goodbye and I left as the newest member of the Faith Relations Committee.

I WASN'T READY

I was excited about the possibilities for this committee, whose primary task was creating a connection between churches and the agency, bringing the faith community back to a faith-based non-profit organization. Quite a task, since the agency had been functioning like a business for several years, but critical because faith was at the core of this agency's mission.

I showed up to committee meetings pumped up and ready to help. Most of the tasks involved identifying individual church leaders for the Executive Director to meet with, or better yet to share the agency's mission with the entire church during one of their services.

This was a little out of my comfort zone, since my only interaction with churches was as a child and through sporadic attendance at our current family church. I attempted to be resourceful, looking for other creative ways to help, but it only took a few months before it became crystal clear why I had been placed on the committee.

The task of connecting with church communities was not only critical but also a larger undertaking for an Executive Director managing an agency amidst change. She was looking for someone she could trust to go out and speak to church congregations... and she apparently found that person in me. My lack of church involvement historically was not a coincidence. In my past, I had several experiences where I felt judged while in a church environment which deterred me. But I thought, "Hey, this must be my opportunity to work through all that and find the place of balance to embrace my faith." So for the second time I wholeheartedly trusted her and said yes. Thinking about the task ahead gave me a large amount anxiety, though, so I would breathe it out, convincing myself this entire process was about growth.

The time finally came for my training. The first step was simple. I was to attend a church service and watch the Director share the message. That was it – all I had to do was show up.

I could give you a long list of excuses, starting with the fact that this first step was asked of me right after I found out my marriage was possibly ending. But regardless, that Sunday morning rolled around and I could not make myself go.

I got ready. I paced. I breathed into the anxiety I was feeling, and the cry of the Banshee appeared again, grieving my moment's incapacity.

You could call me a coward. I certainly felt like one. Unable to compose myself, knowing that I would be unable to confront her without falling to pieces, I sent an email apologizing for my unexpected absence and said that due to some personal issues I needed to step down temporarily from the committee.

As much as I recognized the growth that was happening within me, it was too fast and I wasn't ready for it. I didn't close the door completely; I left it cracked. Every once in a while, I take a peek and see if maybe it's time, but I still haven't gone back. That door of opportunity is still waiting to be opened in the future.

Opportunities surround us every day, and we are given this beautiful gift of free will that allows us to decide whether or not to take them. We are given the power to decide how much discomfort we are willing to endure. We are able to control the speed of the path, both a blessing and a curse.

Avoiding the uncomfortable feels safe,
but it is the discomfort that is necessary
to get us to where we want to be.

Dreams are made of discomfort and it is a journey. Discomfort will always exist, but so will new levels of comfort. Before we close the book on examples of this shift, I need to share one more with you.

Not Mine

Opportunities sometimes present themselves in a manner that seems so obvious and relevant to what we are seeking, however, patience has taught me that sometimes opportunities and signs are not meant for you.

We have the ability to be the vehicle that helps move others towards their doors of opportunity, and to hold their hand as they walk through. This last story is not mine; it is my husband's, and if we had not walked through this door together, Leadership Arts Associates would not exist today.

My husband tasked me to come up with a business plan if I were to do full-time consulting. The template I found courtesy of Microsoft was daunting and I felt like I was just making crap up to fill in the blanks. I had no idea about services, fees, and target audience. I treated the plan like a college research paper and trusted Google search to guide me.

As part of the process, Josh wanted me to meet with a competitor and discuss the viability of my business model. I reached out to a couple of my professional colleagues. Most were reluctant or super secretive when it came to dishing about current business practices.

My husband, who has always classified me as a corporate trainer, reached out to a local organization that had high success facilitating sales training. He asked if I would be open to meeting with them. I agreed as long as he would come with me, since...

...This whole thing was his idea.

Josh knew this man, who I had never met before. His contact surprisingly was more than happy to meet with me. Once again, I entered a meeting with no preparation because I wasn't entirely sure why I was there.

After introductions, the three of us got situated in this gentleman's office, Josh sitting next to me and the mystery man sitting across the way. He nodded, as though a signal to start, and I was lost. I didn't know what the point of the meeting was, so I was brutally honest.

I told the story of how we had gotten to that moment. Josh added some clarifying comments about what he was hoping to achieve. The man then turned to ask me what I wanted to do. I still had no idea, I just shared what I knew. I shared about what I thought was the industry need and where I thought I could make a difference.

Instead of responding to me, the gentleman smiled and turned towards Josh. He said, "We aren't here for her. We are here because you need to know if she can do this. You need to know that you aren't simply blind by love, and that she actually has what it takes. I don't know your wife, but from what I've heard in the last 10 minutes and what I see in her eyes when she shares it... she has it."

I was stunned. The meeting had definitely taken a turn I never saw coming. We left that day both certain that this new business venture was the next step. I quit my job that week.

An amazing powerful experience that was not meant for me, but for my husband... I still get chills whenever I begin to doubt this business endeavor that I have taken on. The doors of opportunity show up to all of us to provide the next lesson needed to reach our dreams.

I wish I could assure you and say the doors get easier, but honestly, I think more and more of these doors show up that you'll want to leave cracked and peek in on occasion. The trick is being able to recognize the lessons of growth and maturity, and not feel like it's karma, or some great vendetta against you.

We can embrace this line of thinking when we remove ourselves from the experience and allow it to drive us to the place we need to reach to listen and learn. This is the last and most powerful exposure I was subjected to during this time – the separation of self.

EXPOSED IN THIS CHAPTER:

1. It becomes a slap in the face, when you realize that perhaps what you wanted is not what you are quite ready for.
2. There are numerous doors presented to us every day. These doors are not so easily spotted, especially if we are allowing life to whisk away at lightning speed.
3. Opportunities surround us every day, and we are given this beautiful gift of free will that allows us to decide whether or not to take them.
4. We are given the power to decide how much discomfort we are willing to endure.
5. Discomfort will always exist, but so will new levels of comfort.
6. The doors of opportunity show up to all of us to provide the next lesson needed to reach our dreams.
7. The trick is being able to recognize the lessons of growth and maturity, and not feel like it's karma, or some great vendetta against you.

CHAPTER 7

THE SEPARATION OF SELF

When it comes to parenting we are typically our worst critic. Personally I never quite know what I'm doing and hope that I'm doing what's best for my children. However, for the most part this judgment happens internally, with the occasional exception of a close friend and relative maybe disagreeing over your nutritional beliefs. But on this day, I experienced a judgment that went way beyond the exception and it happened with a perfect stranger.

IS THIS REALLY HAPPENING?

Upon picking up my six year old from daycare, my husband discovered that Maddy was not herself. She was in visible pain saying that her right ear hurt, as a result of a little boy yelling into it very loudly during snack time. She had been battling a summer cold over the previous two weeks and we thought she had successfully made it through. But her obvious pain and visible exhaustion showed the signs of an ear infection. Our pediatrician would be unable to see Maddy until the following day so we decided to take her to a local urgent care center that accepts walk-ins. I had used it countless times before, though it was actually on the farthest end of town from us. Regardless, I made the drive because the people who worked there were always so wonderful with my children.

When we arrived, there was no visible line and the lady at check-in was able to register us immediately. I told Maddy to take a seat nearby, hoping that she might be a bit more comfortable. She looked absolutely miserable.

While I was finishing up registering her, another family arrived. Out of the entire empty waiting room they decided to sit in the row across from Maddy. I was watching my daughter pretty intently, making sure that she was okay and as comfortable as possible. I could hear the mother of the newly seated family making small talk with Maddy. She asked her what was wrong and what hurt.

Maddy cuddled even more so under her blanket, but being the trooper she is, she attempted to answer those countless questions even if it was just a nod.

The mother was then called to check-in at another window. When she got up she made a comment that Maddy should press charges. I smiled assuming my daughter had told her about the boy at school. After I finished registering, I sat in the chair next to Maddy, feeling completely helpless. I hoped we would soon be called to go back to be seen.

The other mother returned shortly as well. I casually smiled at her, wanting to send a non-verbal thank you for being so caring to my sick child in the waiting room. However, her response was unexpected. She stared right at me and said, "Disgusting." She then continued to make comments along the lines of "certain people just shouldn't have children," and that she would never yell at her children so loudly their ears hurt as a result. She then reiterated to her children how much she loves them, and how other people don't love their children as much. In between this commentary she kept repeating "disgusting," and simply glared at me.

After it became clear she was not going to stand down, I finally engaged and asked, "What?" Her quick response was, "You know what. *You* disgust me. I would never bring my child to the doctor and sit here innocently when it was my fault she was here in pain in the first place."

In that moment, I realized where her anger stemmed from. She thought I hurt my child, that I caused her pain. She had judged me. Her eyes were filled with anger and hatred. She believed I was a child abuser. The woman continued getting louder, making remarks that someone should call the cops and report me to child services. But no one in the office seemed to react to the woman. In fact, everyone around me acted like they were completely unaware of what was happening. I was left to endure the judgment, hatred, and anger alone. I was also left to somehow provide a level of comfort and safety to my six year old in these uncertain and pretty much unbelievable circumstances.

But what happened next caught me off guard. Her judgments drove me inward and caused me to question why her opinion of me mattered so much, or even at all. Her accusations couldn't have been more untrue at face value. However, the underlying messages being sent along with her accusation presented some truth. Deep down, I believed that I was a bad mother.

I began to ask myself if I was doing enough as a mother. I started to question if I was being the mother that I wanted to be to my children. I started to question and check in with my priorities.

I used this situation and removed the sense of attack to transform it into a period of reflection for myself. I was able to quiet the inner chatter typically triggered by our protective system – better known as getting defensive – to be able to listen to what was actually happening inside me.

Unusual and Unexpected

After sharing this experience with multiple people, I found that my ability to tune out those defensive reflexes was not very common. Most people said that if it had been them, they would have given that lady a piece of their mind. One person even said they would have punched her in the face. Regardless, the common thread is that most would engage and escalate the situation.

I can completely relate to this reaction, because once upon a time that would have been my reaction as well. This was the first situation I'd encountered that showed me how far I had come personally. In a moment of attack, I was able to see the lesson about myself and not instantly defer blame to the other individual.

As backwards as it may sound, over the years I have come to learn and appreciate that the more messed up a situation is... the greater the lesson. It also appears that if we fail to listen or recognize the lessons we need to learn, the situations presented become bigger and more of a spectacle, almost like the universe is screaming for your attention.

See, this lesson of exploring my new identity as a mother had come up several times before, yet each time it presented itself, I chose to process it at face value or barely scratch the surface. In fact, three years prior, the same lesson presented itself in a much more reasonable fashion. I even woke up and paid attention briefly, so much so that I wrote about it. This blog article was one of my first ever as a new business owner and to date is still one of my most successful posts.

THE BLOG POST

Wednesday, I got the dreaded phone call from my daughter's daycare. Folks with children can probably relate: the call informs you that your child has a fever and must be picked up immediately, and cannot return until not having a fever for 24 hours. This phone call always equals frustration and anxiety. It literally translates as: plan on leaving work early today, plan on not being at work tomorrow and possibly the day after, decide if your child must see the doctor and/or find a sitter for the times that you have a previous engagement that you cannot get out of.

Now I know I might have a mild form of obsessive-compulsive behavior. I like to plan. Specifically, I like to know how much time I have available to complete my tasks and projects. When that time is snatched away in a manner that is beyond my control, I enter Camp Unhappy.

After spending an afternoon in Camp Unhappy, I reflected that evening on how I got there and why. Frankly, the result of my reflection was that I was disgusted with myself. When examining the facts, I had become upset because I had to leave work to take care of my baby girl – my bundle of joy who was sick and needed her mommy. Why did this upset me? Because it disrupted my plans?

The following day, I attended the only previous engagement that I needed to be at, while my sick little girl stayed with her Lola (aka Grandma). I got into a conversation with someone about generations. Now conversations about generations are typically the norm for me, since it's been a hot topic lately. Yet this discussion somehow shifted to work-life balance. The individual I was talking with stated how she respected a particular generation's views of work-life balance. In particular their ability to let it go... to leave work at work and come home to truly "be" with their family. Not just physically home while mentally still working.

I believe that there are no coincidences and things happen for a reason. People are placed in your path and say things at specific times for a reason. It's up to us to be open and ready-minded to learn the lesson. This moment, quite frankly, was a slap in the face for me. One large reason I was starting my business was in order to have the freedom to create an organization I believed in 100%, and putting family first was a value I planned to instill within my company. Here we were a week away from my Grand Opening and I was already slipping.

Now I ask you, what is your work-life balance situation like? Does it need an adjustment? Perhaps not a major adjustment, just a minor one like mine?

Work-life balance is such a buzzword right now, yet we need to figure out what it means for us individually. What I need in my life to maintain my work-life balance is different than what you need. Regardless, it's important to get a pulse on exactly what this balance is. Ask yourself, is the balance you have the one you are seeking? How does your current balance align with your priorities?

No Such Thing as Coincidences

If you remember in the first story I shared with you, the word that woman repeatedly used to describe me was "disgusting." In the blog post written three years prior, I wrote that I was "disgusted" with myself.

This woman and her blatant confrontation was my own shadow confronting me.

The shadows I see in you reflect
the shadows I see within me.
The light I see in you reflects
the light I see within me.

I needed to answer the question for myself: Why am I disgusted with myself as a mother? This question is not very comfortable to process. In fact, my role and identity as a mother is probably one of the most, if not *the* most vulnerable one I hold as an individual. This explains why I needed a universe smackdown moment.

Regardless of how unpleasant it is, I have found that the lessons which result in monumental growth are typically the most uncomfortable. They are also the ones we frequently attempt to avoid. This only results in them materializing in more and more ways, giving us the feeling that we are surrounded, trapped, and unable to escape. But we totally can. The escape route is within you. So, think on this the next time you're asking, "Why does this keep happening to me?"

REASONABLE EXPECTATIONS

Recently I was teaching a workshop in which a participant asked for further clarification. The person said that when they heard me apply the concepts to my own life it made perfect sense, but when they attempted to apply it to their own they got lost.

The example I used above is extreme for sure. If, as you read the story, you were thinking, *"There is no way I could ever be in a place where I could separate myself from the moment and learn a lesson about myself,"* I totally get it! That was me at one point, too.

I share it because it's possible. I am not some sort of super human or spiritual guru. I am mortal, living my life one day at a time like everyone else, but the way we live it can be different and it is moments like these that can change everything.

EXPOSED IN THIS CHAPTER:

1. The more messed up a situation is... the greater the lesson.
2. If we fail to listen or recognize the lessons we need to learn, the situations presented become bigger and more of a spectacle, almost like the universe is screaming for your attention.
3. People are placed in your path and say things at specific times for a reason. It's up to us to be open and ready-minded to learn the lesson.
4. The lessons which result in monumental growth are typically the most uncomfortable.
5. The escape route is within you.

CHAPTER 8

THE POWER OF TIME

My exposure moments are pretty average on the grand scale of possible life events. But they were ugly and uncomfortable, all the ingredients needed to facilitate a shift on my path to personal transformation.

I encountered at least five shifts that I just shared with you, though there certainly are more. Those were the five that were alive and at work in my life. For me these shifts, despite the vulnerable state I personally had to reach to achieve them, were necessary to completely transform me one step forward on my path.

That's right. I said forward. One step forward.

As these moments were happening around me, even after I was exposed to *The Slight Edge* philosophy, my first instinct was still to believe that life was happening against me... that karma from all my juvenile decisions was catching up to me and now I was going to crash and burn.

What a toxic philosophy, to believe that if we are not perfect or exceeding expectations – set by ourselves or others – that we deserve to be punished for the rest of our life. I know I am not alone in believing in this toxic philosophy, whether you want to articulate it or not.

KARMA

The Slight Edge was the first educational method that successfully taught me the power of compound interest. I still remember my lightbulb moment. I was so excited I had to share my newfound knowledge with my husband. Yes, my husband the Financial Advisor. He rolled his eyes and said, "It took a book for you to understand that? We've talked about this before."

Clearly, I hadn't listened or wasn't paying attention. Perhaps it hadn't been my time to learn that lesson until now. The compound-interest lightbulb resonated so strongly with me because of its direct correlation to time. Sure, the connection made perfect sense in terms of finances, but it was the concept of compounding time that made me see other things differently.

According to Dictionary.com, *karma* has the following four definitions:

- Action, seen as bringing upon oneself inevitable results, good or bad, either in this life or in a reincarnation.
- The cosmic principle according to which each person is rewarded or punished in one

incarnation according to that person's deed in the previous incarnation.

- Fate; destiny.
- The good or bad emanations felt to be generated by someone or something.

By this definition, karma is much larger than how we commonly choose to recognize it in our culture. In contrast, UrbanDictionary.com defines it as:

- Getting what you give, or reaping what you sow.
- Whatever you do comes back to you.
- Cause and effect. From good living, we become a better person, gain greater inner peace, and enjoy a good life. From bad living, we become a worse person, destroying our inner peace and becoming plagued by a bad life. Simple as that.

But if these latter definitions of karma are the truth we hold, we need to recognize the dependency on "right" and "wrong," "good" and "bad." Where do those definitions come from?

Sure, there are certain things we can probably universally agree are good and right, or bad and wrong. However, our daily lives are filled with decisions that can only be answered by our own personal compass. The definitions of good and bad, right and wrong, are the ones we personally believe. And this dictates whether we feel karma is coming into play. Our expectation of ourselves, which are comprised of outside influences, is the truth that we hold.

At first glance, I thought the concepts of *compounding time* and *karma* were the same. What I soon realized is that I was basing my beliefs on the narrower UrbanDictionary.com definition. Karma in its larger meaning refers to the life we choose to lead. It is not based on every unmet expectation of ourselves.

Life is full of lessons. Some are celebratory in nature and others are difficult, materializing as loss or failure. Those are the lessons that, if we pay attention, will empower us to live in alignment with the life we want to lead. If that's a life of doing good or being bad, that's when karma will come into play.

But until that time, the compounding effect is at play and it is what makes time so powerful. The compounding effect of our daily decisions is what generates our daily outcomes. These daily decisions and outcomes then impact the next day's and the day after that. This is our ability to make time work for us... or against us.

WORKING FOR ME, AGAINST ME, OR BEING STUBBORN

We have the ability with every decision we make to choose to have time work for us or against us. Knowing that time doesn't stop for anyone, we know our decisions will eventually have one of two outcomes – promote us or expose us. Every decision is included in this equation.

My favorite example of this compounding effect is the king-sized Snickers candy bar. If I decide today to adopt a daily practice of enjoying one, it will not expose me immediately. The outside world will not know on Day One that I have made this decision. Inside, I may realize it's not the best or healthiest choice for myself, but externally I will not see any physical change.

As I continue this new daily practice, the outside world and my external self may not even see it after a month. There isn't even a guarantee that you'll be exposed at the one-year mark. However, you know inside this is a decision that is working against you and the life you want to lead. The tricky thing about time is that it doesn't tell you when it will happen... but there is a guarantee that if you continue this habit, it will expose you.

It may be through excessive weight gain or the development of a health issue. It could also be a change in personal energy flow and capability. At that point when time starts to expose you, the outside world will begin to notice. Then the question always becomes: *How hard is it to get back into alignment afterward?* Whatever time frame you've spent establishing this habit has been working against you and what you want. How long will it take you to reverse it?

I love this example because it talks about the power of a snack, but since I have shared the vulnerable story with you regarding my own Snickers habit, you know that I personally was exposed as the result.

That is an exposure which I am still undoing. It has a snowball effect. Not only does compounding time allow us to cement the daily practice of self-sabotage, but we become in alignment with that negative state of mind. As a result, all of these decisions move us further away from the life we want to lead, further out of alignment.

All along, I thought time was working against me, however I now believe it's more like I was just stubborn. In order for time to truly work against you, you have to want it to. You have to be actively seeking self-sabotage. For most of us though, it's more likely that we don't want to believe in ourselves.

Strong self-esteem can be so foreign to us that we choose to live out of alignment, and as a result time continues to move forward, exposing us in necessary ways to grow – the growth that is necessary to promote us to the life we want and were meant to lead.

I know I am not alone in being stubborn. Many of us choose to not see the path we are currently on, or even acknowledge the path we *could* be on. Therefore, more than once you have to be blatantly shown. This is time exposing you with the intent to promote you.

WHAT'S NEXT

Now that I have shared my moments of exposure and resulting shifts towards transformation that occurred, I want to show you how to begin the same transformation process for yourself. The beauty of this process is that it will meet you exactly where you are at that moment. These five shifts will adapt to your level, so then you can continue to push them further to maximize your transformation... what I like to call an *aligned life* – a life that is fulfilling, abundant, and purposeful.

I personally call this my *HRart*. I will explain why in Part Two, but right now to get you started in the transformation process I would like to introduce the Rollercoaster Reflection.

The Rollercoaster Reflection is a visual timeline of your life. I prefer to use the imagery associated with a rollercoaster because life is full of ups, downs, hidden drops, sudden turns, and loops. This specific exercise will utilize a technique I call the "controlled scribble."

The main goal of this exercise is to scribble a rollercoaster track that represents your life during the time you believe you were being exposed. There are two ways to complete this exercise. The first is to listen to my guided visualization audio track (available for download at: sammsmeltzer.com/book). On that track, I will walk you through the exercise step by step. Or if that doesn't float your boat at the moment, you can follow the written steps listed below.

THE ROLLERCOASTER REFLECTION

1. Grab a piece of paper (the bigger the better) and a pen (or pencil, marker, crayon, etc.).
2. Close your eyes and think back to a time when you felt exposed. This moment will serve as your starting point.
3. Place your pen to the paper and create a line that aligns with how you felt in that moment of exposure (down, up, sudden fall, loop).
4. Then think of the next exposure moment that occurred after the first one, and create a line that represents that exposure moment's feeling.

Continue steps 3 and 4 until you feel your track is complete in representing the timeframe you believe you should be processing right now.

A few things to keep in mind as you complete this reflection:

- The initial moment that you identify is the starting point of the timeframe you are meant to process right now. Trust yourself.
- If this is proving challenging, and you find yourself questioning whether you are doing it right, you are overthinking the process. Once again, trust yourself. What feels right is right.
- When attempting to determine when the exercise is complete, the answer lies in... yes, trusting yourself. When it feels complete, it is.

This exercise will serve you greatly as you start Part II and begin your own path of transformation.

Set your outcomes from this exercise aside until I call for you to reference it in Part Two.

EXPOSED IN THIS CHAPTER:

1. The exposure moments are ugly and uncomfortable, but are the ingredients needed to facilitate a shift on the path of personal transformation.
2. A toxic philosophy is to believe that we are not perfect or exceeding expectations – set by ourselves or others. As a result, we believe we deserve to be punished for the rest of our life.
3. Our expectations of ourselves, which are comprised of outside influences, are the truths that we hold.
4. Karma in its larger meaning refers to the life we choose to lead. It is not based on every unmet expectation of ourselves.
5. The compounding effect of our daily decisions is what generates our daily outcomes. These daily decisions and outcomes then impact the next day's and the day after that. This our ability to make time work for us... or against us.
6. Strong self-esteem can be so foreign to us that we choose to live out of alignment.
7. An abundant life is a life that is fulfilling, abundant and purposeful.
8. Trust yourself. What feels right is right. The answer lies in you.

PART TWO

EXPOSING YOU

CHAPTER 9

*Our culture pushes us to jump straight to
solutions. We want the "how-to" without taking
time to identify if we are even ready for it.*

AM I READY?

Just as Part One was about me, Part Two is focused
on you. In this section I will give you the first steps
in each of the concentrated foundational areas to
start moving you in the right directions. These
exercises are several of the most popular I use with
my coaching clients today, and though you may be
curious, you might still find you are wrestling with
internal resistance.

You may be asking yourself: *Am I ready for this?
Does any of this even apply to me?* Well, let me
assure you that the structure of this book is
intentional. I chose purposely to not provide any of
the experiential lessons until Part Two because I
needed to first share with you *why* the experiential
lessons are significant.

SAMM SMELTZER

These lessons will manifest within each of us differently and even though you may not have had experiences that closely resemble what I shared, more than likely they reminded you of something from your own life. It was this connection that continued to propel you forward throughout the chapters to where you are now. This should serve as affirmation that you are exactly where you need to be. I don't care where you are in your career or life at this moment, these foundational transformational shifts will serve you.

The one confirmation I see time and time again from my clients that lets me know they are ready for this work is that they have all had a *stirring* occur. A stirring is what I define as an event or sequence of events that lead to a moment where the individual can separate themselves from what is happening, and recognize some element of what's going on. This is my cue that you have had an awakening on the self-awareness spectrum and therefore will be open to increasing your awareness further.

Now before you go thinking that a *stirring* is some big dramatic moment in your life, it can technically manifest more like a blip.

Let me give you an example of a stirring I witnessed, and this individual still doesn't know it happened. Ian was part of one of my mutual professional circles. Through a common connection I was recommended to meet with him because of his new business venture and how his services would benefit my professional endeavors. During our meeting, I

118

was in business-boss-lady mode attempting to understand all the ins, outs, and fees associated with his service, because I was actually highly interested in what he had to offer.

Randomly throughout our conversation, Ian said three times in different ways, "I need your help." I don't remember the context or the exact words, but to me I heard, "I need your help" loud and clear. After the third time, I put down my pen from my notes and said, "Why do you keep saying that?" He replied, "I don't know. I just do."

I probed a bit more and learned that Ian had quite a few business endeavors happening, and he had recently transitioned from another industry. He mentioned that he was overwhelmed with the financial pressures of life but affirmed that he felt like he was on the right path professionally and enjoyed what he did. He then went back to his initial response of, "I don't know but I feel like something is missing."

This was confirmation that a stirring has occurred. For Ian to know something was missing, he had to have processed an event or sequence of events where he was able to remove himself. It is a bit of a strange concept, but a powerful one. I left Ian by encouraging him to explore that feeling more, and when he found himself feeling like something was lacking, to challenge himself to answer the question, "What?"

If you were able to connect with any story that I shared in Part One, then that is confirmation that you too have experienced a *stirring...* and you are ready.

THE PATH

There are five Ps on this path:

1. Purpose
2. Passion
3. People
4. Possibility
5. Power

Each "P" represents a foundational lesson. These lessons do not have a specific order that they need to occur in, however I have listed them here by order of difficulty, based on what I have observed through my work.

Each chapter includes a lesson I typically share with clients who have reached this point in their path, then ends with an experiential exercise that can be completed to begin foundational transformation.

A JOURNAL

These five foundational lessons are all about high levels of success and low stress. In order to achieve this, I am recommending that you dedicate a journal to record and log this journey. Journals can be powerful learning tools, if used correctly. Your journal should be used intentionally to capture thoughts, feelings, needs, and desires relative to this journey. Try to steer clear of using it for venting or mindless doodles.

You can complete a journal entry at any time on this journey. The exercises included in this portion of the book can take individuals as little as one hour to complete or as long as a year. The best gauge to know whether or not to complete a journal entry is your reactive emotional intensity to the circumstances. Whether it is a positive or negative emotional reaction if it is highly intensive, it is worthy of an entry. In addition, the more entries you do, the better possible growth outcome awaits.

Journal entries for this purpose should include:

- Date
- Title that identifies the circumstances that triggered the entry
- 1-2 minutes of writing that answers one or all of the following questions: What are you thinking? What are you feeling? What are you needing? What are you wanting?

To practice, let's utilize your Rollercoaster Reflection from the end of Part One.

1. Write today's date in your journal.
2. Title the entry Rollercoaster Reflection.
3. Write for 1-2 minutes about what you are thinking, feeling, wanting, or needing as a result of the Rollercoaster Reflection.

The Rollercoaster Reflection was your first exposure exercise and it gave you a preview into a timeframe that may be a good starting place for you to begin this journey. It also possibly highlighted life events that you will want to explore further in Part Two. It might be best to keep your Rollercoaster Reflection close by as you move onward.

CHAPTER 10

IN THIS LESSON, WE WILL:

- Explore the significance of exposing your purpose
- Discuss how your purpose may materialize
- Complete a visualization exercise to begin exposing your purpose

Estimated Time to Complete this Lesson: 1 Hour

EXPOSING PURPOSE

To expose our purpose, we must be selfish. The biggest hurdle I have seen for so many is their inability to gain clarity of their purpose. This stems from a continual allowance of outside influence. We are influenced externally by so many forces from a very early age – parents, teachers, friends, bosses, spouses, our children, and the list goes on and on. With so many outside influences easily accessible, it becomes almost natural to get caught up in the noise, becoming completely disconnected with the voice within that guides us to our calling.

That's right: *calling*. We all have one. It is the reason or intention for our existence, and despite whatever faith background you come from, the internal compass that you know is within you should serve as affirmation. There is more to life than simply birth, everything in-between, and death. It is this something *more* that serves as an innate motivation to wake up every morning and trudge ahead when life gets hard.

NOT SO SIMPLE

After lots of internal work, I am finally able to articulate my purpose. My purpose is that...

I am a healer. I am a teacher.

These two simple sentences were not exposed so simply. When I first started to seek, to get clear on my purpose, it truly was like an expedition. Every experience or moment that I processed provided some other new hint or clue to my greater aspiration. The exercise for this lesson will give you just that – a new nugget to add in your journey to clarity. This exercise will not provide your purpose to you in a simple sentence as mine is recorded above. However, I think it is important to know how a purpose can be articulated to have an idea of what the end goal might look like.

That's right, *might*. There is no one-size-fits-all formula. Your purpose will be articulated in a manner that makes sense to you, and it only has to make sense to you. My two sentences are crystal clear to me, while to you they may seem confusing and overly vague. The beauty about our own personal purpose is that it serves only one individual. You.

PURPOSEFUL PRACTICE

The exercise for this lesson is a guided visualization. As I mentioned before, the 5 P's do not have to be completed in any particular order. But I have placed them specifically in an order in this book, by the relative difficulty level of these experiential exercises.

A guided visualization exercise is a great place to begin for two reasons:

1. It is 100% guided and requires no additional materials. That means you simply play the audio track, listen, and experience.
2. It is purposeful practice in quieting the mind. The more comfortable and effective you become at quieting your mind, the more effective these exercises will be for you.

A RETURN TO CHILDHOOD

The visualization is titled *Inner Child, Inner Joy*, and it is all about returning to a point in childhood where you were naive. A time when you were not yet able to fully welcome the external influences surrounding you, when you could easily refocus on the voice inside and be in your own little world.

In Chapter 4, I account for the path of exposure moments that began to lead me back to this inner child. It was the last place where I could recollect feeling like my true authentic self. It was these exposure moments that began to shine the light on the magnitude of the influence others have had on my path. I had essentially been detoured, so this gave me a serious wake-up call on how much I needed to backtrack.

Those initial exposure moments accounted for the first steps in that backtracking which eventually reunited me with myself. I needed to know what I needed to be... me, successfully... and believe that I was worthy of a purpose. It almost served as the prerequisite in my purpose conquest.

WHAT TO EXPECT

The expected outcomes from this exercise are varied. It could materialize like my initial exposure moments – a sign that some pre-work is needed. It could also materialize in a different manner. Here are two materializations I have found to be common outcomes.

1) *An indirect return to childhood or a more youthful you*

Tom came to experience this visualization exercise as a client of curiosity. This means he solely became my client because he was curious about the services I offered. He was a mutual professional connection and wanted to gain a greater understanding of my business so he could help me grow. His sense of genuine curiosity allowed him to enter every exercise openly and willingly. After listening to the guided visualization, Tom shared that he went immediately to his childhood home and remembered his childhood street. He continued to share that this home had obvious significance to him but in addition to that, it also was the street where he and his wife had both coincidentally lived before initially connecting. Tom was a realtor who had lost his wife a few years prior and was now discovering a life on his own.

As a coach, part of my responsibility when working with clients is both to listen to what the client is saying, and also to listen to what is *not* being said... what we call the *unsaid.*

What I heard in Tom's voice as he shared was destiny. Tom was hinting at the sense of destiny which surrounded the way he and his wife had met. In addition, the fact that he instantly went to a place that emphasized the concept of home (especially given his chosen industry), there was a sort of affirmation and destiny to his professional path as well. Whether Tom understood this intricacy or not, I could tell that an affirmation of some sort had materialized within him.

2) *Less seeing and more feeling*

Courtney experienced the visualization exercise at the same time as Tom. They were in a group session together and Courtney had registered after seeing a random social media post. From the beginning of our time together, Courtney's uncertainty was evident. However, below that uncertainty was a true desire to be open and willing to the experience. After completing the exercise, Courtney got the opportunity to first hear Tom share his outcomes. Courtney was initially hesitant about sharing what she saw because she was disheartened that she hadn't seen a childhood memory. With the exercise's title *Inner Child, Inner Joy*, she assumed that not seeing her childhood meant failure in regard to the exercise.

Let me assure you, there is no way you can fail at this. This exercise will materialize for you the way it must to start laying the foundation for clarity in regard to your purpose. To shut down this negative self-talk, I quickly asked Courtney what she saw. She shared that she was in a meadow with her own children, though the meadow didn't really serve any sort of reminiscent significance. She started to dig to see if there was some distant meadow memory that would justify why it was her outcome. While she was digging she continued to share verbally what a meadow symbolized to her, and how she felt in the moment. The *unsaid* that occurred here is that Courtney's outcome was about the feeling, the sensation that was given to her as a result of that imagery represents the feeling that will be given to her as a result of her purpose.

Feelings are powerful cues and hints. Now that Courtney is familiar with the feeling associated with her purpose, she can more likely identify it in her daily life. This means that decisions and actions which align with her purpose will give her this feeling, and therefore it will be easy for her to find reassurance that she is on the right path. The next step for Courtney is continuing the work of identifying her purpose so she can articulate it.

YOUR TURN

Are you ready to find out your outcomes from this visualization exercise? Before you listen to the audio track, make sure you have found a spot where you won't be disturbed. It works more effectively if your eyes can be closed and you can focus on the guiding direction provided, therefore I highly recommend you *not* complete this exercise while driving.

Instead, complete the exercise sitting in a chair, on the ground, or even laying down... whatever you are comfortable with. Other than that, enjoy!

You can download this visualization exercise at sammsmeltzer.com/book. I have also included the transcript for the visualization exercise on the following pages.

INNER CHILD, INNER JOY

Get comfortable in your chair, feet flat on the ground.

Your hands rest comfortably in your lap, on your knees or at your sides.

Sit up tall with shoulders relaxed. Make sure they aren't creeping up to your ears.

Now close your eyes and begin focusing on your breath.

Create a breath that comes from your belly.

As you inhale, feel your belly rise, and then on the exhale feel the release.

Let's take a few more deep breaths in a row.

Right now, it is just you and your breath – the rest of the world is melting away.

Any surrounding sounds or distractions slip farther and farther into the distance eventually fading away.

It is just you and your breath.

In the darkness of having your eyes gently closed, shapes begin to take form.

At first glance, they are unrecognizable and a blur of moving shapes and colors.

As they begin to settle down, the shapes become clearer and you now know it is a silhouette of someone walking towards you.

Each step brings them closer to you and with each step, you take in a little more detail of this visitor.

You then realize that this person walking towards you is you.

A much younger you but still most definitely you.

A you that knew the world before judgement and expectations.

A you where imagination and possibility are a daily way of life.

A you that lives a life of joy that you have forgotten, though maybe not completely.

But you know you don't remember it completely either. It is a piece that somehow got left behind.

This *little you* now stands before you, staring up at you – curious and even a bit naive.

In these eyes, you can tell instantly that they don't have a real care, concern, or stress in their little world right now.

They feel safe, protected, free to dream, free to be happy.

The youth of you is now turning away and begins to move in another direction. You move with that youth now curious too.

As you move together, around you are new but familiar surroundings. You know this place well. It was a place you came often in your mind as a child in the world of pretend and play.

Perhaps it is a classroom and you're ready to teach, a patient's room and you're ready to suit up in the white coat, or a packed stadium arena waiting for you to take stage.

This is a place that you love, a place you couldn't wait to return to.

Pause a moment and take it in, take in these surroundings that may seem from so long ago. What calls to you, what do you notice, how do you feel?

Explore and take in the beautiful details created by your mind that have been here all this time.

Embrace why this place made you so happy and brought you so much joy. Appreciate the level of peace and satisfaction that comes just from being present.

Now it is time to go find little you, find them and say thank you. Thank you for the reminder and gift of never forgetting.

Thank you for keeping this place safe which has been dormant for so long in your mind.

Thank you for reminding me of this feeling that resonates within.

Thank you for connecting me back to the possibility that I need to find that joy and peace I am seeking.

As the place begins to fade away into the background, you know it is time to now say goodbye. But remember that this place is here for you whenever you want to return. Because this place is yours and it was created just for moments like this.

Bring your attention back to your breath.

As your breathing returns to normal, become aware of the room again.

Know where you are, maybe start moving your head side to side or wiggling your fingers, and when you are ready, open your eyes.

COMPLETING THIS LESSON:

- Complete the visualization exercise.
- In your journal, free write any thoughts or feelings you have after completing the exercise. This may include noting what you experienced personally.
- Close by answering two questions: In this moment, what do you want right now? In this moment, what do you need right? You can record your response to these questions in your journal as well.

CHAPTER 11

In This Lesson, We Will:

- Explore the significance of passion
- Discuss how passion is typically identified through signs
- Complete an exercise to find your sign and expose your passion

Estimated Time to Complete this Lesson: 1 Week

Exposing Passion

The dictionary defines passion as a strong and barely controllable emotion. Sound familiar? It should because this definition is almost identical to how I would define my cry of the Banshee. This cry served as my default sign from the universe. But what was typically the trigger that brought forth such a strong and barely controllable emotion was passion. I would not have had such an intense, driving feeling for something or someone I did not care about.

Now I recognize that for some of you, reading Chapter 3 about my cry of the Banshee may have left you perplexed. Perhaps you did a casual scan over your life to see if you'd been dealt a default sign as well that you have somehow managed to neglect. If you found one, that is awesome, but for most people, these signs remain well hidden. In fact, I have yet to find someone who has a similar sign that is traumatizing like my cry of the Banshee.

NEVER FEAR

Just because you don't have a sign that is hanging right below the surface ready to erupt at any given hint of passion, it doesn't mean that you cannot ask for a sign and be shown. In Chapter 3, I mentioned my spiritual mentor, Gabrielle Bernstein, who asks the universe for a sign through specific criteria. For example, "If I am on the right path for my life, let me see a hawk as my sign." Then you might see a hawk flying in the direction you are driving or when you walk into a store, you might notice a small hawk statue.

Choosing your sign, I have found, is a source of discomfort for some who have not done much internal work of this nature. Plus, for those who choose their sign then fail to see it, they become quickly discouraged and skeptical. All the work you do on yourself to gain clarity should move you forward and not backward. My goal is to never give you an exercise that makes you so uncomfortable that you begin to question the process.

The path of self-discovery should be fun and challenging, but it should always make sense to you.

You are the reason for this journey and therefore every outcome solely has to make sense to you.

So to counteract the common initial reactions to choosing your sign. I have now flipped the script, where you participate in the sign finding process, and then when you're ready, reveal the sign's meaning.

NO ONE WAY

This is no different than the guided visualization exercise in the last chapter. You cannot do this wrong. I will share with you the methodology which has proven most effective with my clients, but if you get a gut instinct to take it a different way, go with it. All these exercises are intuitively driven and literally are an exercise for your intuition, to make it stronger and louder. Therefore, if your intuition is pulling you in a different direction, that's what we want, so listen and proceed.

I call this exercise *Seeing It*. Let me forewarn you that it has proven time and again to be powerful in achieving exactly the outcome my clients have been seeking. However, even though the outcome is there, some clients still struggle to see what is in front of them. More pre-work is needed when they aren't in a place to accept what they see. This happens for a variety of reasons. Let me share with you more specifically what I mean.

Claire came to me because her professional life was lacking its previous satisfaction. She would continually articulate that something felt like it was missing, and even more so express that there had to be more out there for her. Her energy overall was heavy, like life had started to take a toll and the years of build-up had gotten her into this place.

Claire and I worked through a series of exercises to expose what mattered most to her and where she needed to focus her energy in order to find that desired fulfillment. Every exercise was delivering the same outcome, but she refused to see it. That's when I improvised and as a result created the "Seeing It" exercise. After completing this exercise, Claire stared at her outcome on the table and couldn't help but be moved to tears. The images that appeared were all of families, and what Claire longed for more than anything else was to be the mother she always wanted to be but never thought she was. At this stage of her life, years away from retirement, time was valuable and she wanted to spend it with those who mattered most.

It was this exercise that resulted in Claire beginning to move forward with clarity that her passion at that moment was her family, and therefore her professional life needed to support that. It became less about the executive level position that took into account all of her experience, and more about the ability to have an 8 to 5, where she could leave work at work and be fully present at home.

How I present the exercise to you below is exactly how Claire completed it. Enjoy!

SEEING IT

Supplies Needed:

- Magazines (that can be destroyed)
- 9" x 12" Manila Envelope

The Process:

1. Set the intention for yourself, either say it out loud or write it down.

I want to expose my passion.

---

2. Then over a 7-day period make an effort to browse a magazine. As you do, tear out any image that speaks to you for any reason. You do not have to be able to articulate that reason. Attempt to stay with images and only pull words or phrases that resonate strongly with you. Place all tear-outs from your browsing session in the manila envelope. Try browsing at different times of day. The more frequently you do this over a period of time, the stronger your outcome will be.

3. Resist the urge over these 7 days to review images you have collected in your envelope. This is a time to collect, not process.

4. After 7 days have passed, find a place where you will be uninterrupted. Review your collection. During this initial review, set aside any images or words that clearly do not resonate or speak as strongly to you as the others. You can then

choose to discard those images or store them in a separate envelope, but do not put them back into your main collection. Return the images you have chosen to keep in your collection back to the envelope.

5. Allow some time to pass before you choose to review the collection again. This could be anywhere from another week to the following day to the next hour. Whatever feels right for you.

6. Remove your images from the envelope and move them around on a flat surface (table, floor, poster board). Set them in an arrangement that feels right. Then look at the images and recognize that this is your passion exposed.

COMPLETING THIS LESSON:

- Set the intention, "I want to expose my passion." This is the simple act of putting it out there, either by saying it out loud or writing it down in your journal.
- For 7 days browse magazines at different times each day.
- Every time you find an image in a magazine that speaks or resonates with you, rip it out and place it in your manila envelope.
- Do not look at the images in your envelope during this time.
- After 7 days, open your envelope and review your images.
- Keep images that most strongly resonate with you.
- Attempt to identify themes or the personal meaning for the images in your final cut.
- In your journal, write any thoughts, feelings, wants, or needs that you have as a result of this exercise.

CHAPTER 12

In This Lesson, We Will:

- Explore how people are our greatest lessons
- Discuss how our personal filters are a source of self-sabotage
- Complete an exercise to identify people who are necessary to expose

Estimated Time to Complete this Lesson: 1 Hour

Exposing People

As I have continued on my path of development, I have found that people are being exposed around me one way or another. Some individuals are being exposed as great supporters and friends, while others are becoming more distant or ingenuine.

> *Your soul*
> *Is attracted to people*
> *The same way flowers*
> *Are attracted to the sun.*
> *Surround yourself*
> *Only with those*
> *Who want to see you grow.*
>
> *~Pavana*

It is easy to think that those who surround us should only be "the light bringers, the magic makers, the world shifters and the game shakers" (Anonymous). But those are not the only individuals who make us grow. They are simply the individuals who provide us with the most pleasant growth experiences. However, it is from interacting with those who prove the most challenging for us that we find a great deal of internal growth.

What we are ultimately seeking is a balance. We do not want one side to become too heavy. At no time should it feel like all your internal development is happening through the light. On the contrary, never should it feel like all your internal development is happening through the shadows. Both have their place.

One of my favorite mantras is...

The light I see in you is a reflection of the light within me.

The shadows I see in you are a reflection of the shadows within me.

WE KNOW WHAT'S BEST

Today it has become almost second nature to pass judgment on others. In a matter of minutes, maybe even in seconds, we believe we know everything about a person. We believe that our own personal filter is best when determining who is worthy to be associated with us, and when we aren't quite confident in that filter we turn to our family and friends to weigh in. It is a constant state of mind that we know what's best for us.

Despite this embraced mindset, so many of us still feel alone. We are lonely and question if we are unwanted.

In one of my employment past lives, I passed a fellow co-worker in the hallway. In our initial interaction, he said hello and I nodded in return. I later learned he had concluded that I thought I was too good for him and this impacted all our future interactions. He was constantly cold to me when I saw him throughout the building. In the lunch room he would come and greet my co-workers but blatantly ignore me. The only reason I knew that he had passed this judgment on me was because I finally asked.

For months, I lived with the cold interactions and it began to taint my entire perspective. I began to believe I was not a good cultural fit for the organization and I wasn't wanted there, and maybe I should leave. These conclusions came as the result of one man and his personal judgment filter.

Was the energy spent on these masquerades valuable? How much conflict is created as a result of masquerades? We believe we know best. In some cases, we even believe we know it all... understand it all... better than anyone else possibly can.

Today, despite my continual attempts to not embrace this judging mindset, it still creeps in. I challenge you to believe the idea, just for a moment, that every person is in your life for a reason. Whether you like them or not, they are there for a reason.

It's Natural

People will come and go, and they should. It is natural. As we grow, we change, as do others, and that includes sometimes outgrowing each other. I believe that people show up when we need them for growth, then after our lesson is learned they either move on in some capacity or grow along with us and become lifelong friends.

The issue arises when an individual should move on but they aren't ready. As a result they hold on. And they hold on for so long – and sometimes so tightly – that they start to contradict their original intention. This can cause us to become stagnant in our own growth, possibly even sending us backwards. This is also the perfect storm to throw someone into a downward spiral that leads to a personal or even professional crash and burn.

So the question then arises, how do we identify these individuals when our personal judgment filters are not always so accurate?

The answer is within you. To assist with hearing this answer, I created the *Toleration Evaluation*.

THE TOLERATION EVALUATION

The Toleration Evaluation is conducted using a mind map, to map out your current tolerations. If you are not familiar with mind maps, I have created a video tutorial and downloadable worksheet you can use to get you started (available at: sammsmeltzer.com/book). Nevertheless, it has been my experience that once people get going with the exercise, the mind map is hard to contain on one sheet of paper.

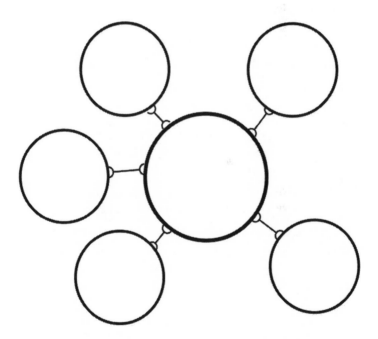

To put it simply, a mind map is a collection of bubbles connected by lines. The lines demonstrate some sort of relationship between the bubbles.

Typically, a mind map begins with a center bubble and all the following bubbles begin to surround it. The center bubble includes the topic or question that the surrounding bubbles will answer.

In my practice, the way the bubbles are connected only has to represent relationships that make sense to the creator. This is typically a technique utilized for brainstorming a topic and that is essentially what we are doing here. We are brainstorming about your life's tolerations.

To get started, the center bubble will serve as you. The bubbles you choose to create around it will represent your current tolerations. A "toleration" can be any sort of rub you are experiencing.

To do this you will be answering the question, *"What am I tolerating today in my life?"*

The phrasing of the question may seem odd. Why ask "what" when we are trying to identify "who"? To put it simply, the phrasing of the question is designed specifically to limit any personal judgment filters you may hold. As I have already mentioned, we all have a tendency to believe that we know what's best. My hope with this exercise is that it reveals the raw authentic answers that will be the most productive to you.

Some of the answers that bubble up may surprise you but put them down on your mind map anyway. Just because they are on the map does not mean you will need to eliminate them. Like I said before, we are looking for a balance. Our primary outcome is to proactively identify those individuals who have perhaps overstayed their welcome.

Once you have finished creating the bubbles of all your current tolerations, the next question to answer is, *"What if I allow this toleration to continue? What will happen to me?"*

Connect a new bubble to all your current tolerations and notate a word or phrase that answers those two questions. It could be anything from ending up emotionally drained, working additional hours, to losing financial security, or even nothing.

The last question you must answer is, *"Who?"*

Who is causing you to tolerate this circumstance? After evaluating each toleration in this fashion, you should be able to identify specific individuals who have overstayed their welcome. The awareness of this alone will prove to be greatly beneficial but the next step is to create an action item or potentially action plan to help them move on.

I recently identified an individual who fell into this category and it was unexpected. I considered this person a friend and had a hard time accepting the idea that she was the cause of me tolerating a particular set of circumstances. I was in so much doubt that my decision to help her move on came in the form of a clarifying conversation. Through this conversation, I shared my tolerations in a hope that it was only a misunderstanding. Instead I was met with blame and resistance. The conversation confirmed, sadly, that this was indeed an individual who needed to move on. She was so taken aback by the conversation that it put this needed step into motion.

Lastly, before we close on this exercise I need to address how to respond if the answer to "who" is you. What this means is that you are currently violating one of your own boundaries and essentially as a result have created a self-sabotaging behavior. This increased awareness is definitely something to be grateful for and signals that an action item or action plan is in order to restore the boundary and move forward.

The Toleration Evaluation only visually depicts what is happening right now in your life. Its intention is to assist you in seeing things more clearly, and possibly through a different lens that will empower you to make the decisions necessary to continue on your path.

COMPLETING THIS LESSON:

- Create a mind map of your answers to the question, "What are you tolerating today?"
- Then add to your mind map, your answers to the following question, "What will happen to me if I allow this to continue?"
- Finally, add to your mind map, your answer to, "Who is the cause of this toleration?"
- In your journal, write any thoughts, feelings, wants, or needs that you have as a result of this exercise.

CHAPTER 13

IN THIS LESSON, WE WILL:

- Define possibilities and opportunities
- Discuss another way our personal filters are a source of self-sabotage
- Establish a practice to begin exposing the full spectrum of possibilities

Estimated Time to Complete this Lesson: 1 Month

EXPOSING POSSIBILITY

Passing judgment on people almost instantly is not the only natural tendency we have developed as a result of the "I know what's best" mindset. You may want to argue with me over the points in the last chapter, thinking if it's true then you are the exception. You are the best gauge of what is good for you, whether that comes to people or opportunities.

You see, it is this same mindset which prevents our capacity to expose possibilities. While this mindset self-sabotages us in both sets of circumstances, what we discussed in regard to people is full of complexities, while in this case it is pretty straight forward. Thinking that you know what's best for you will limit your opportunities because you cannot see the full spectrum of possibilities.

WHAT IS AN OPPORTUNITY?

Maybe the confusion starts with us not fully comprehending what an *opportunity* is. According to the dictionary, an opportunity is a set of circumstances that make it possible to do something. But for many of us, we associate additional criteria with this definition. This additional criteria is our own personal filter to weed out opportunities that our previously mentioned mindset believes are not what's best for us.

Most of my coaching sessions take on this inevitable format, beginning with a complete recap of what has happened since I last saw the client. During this sharing I consistently find myself making notes of missed opportunities. In these scenarios, the client rarely recognizes the circumstances I identify as opportunities, and for most, this is because their personal filter is so strict with super specific criteria.

Pat came to me after he decided to leave his full-time job to pursue opening his own business. One of the big obstacles for Pat in this process was financial security. He did not have the current means to pursue his passionate business venture. His wife earned enough that full-time employment for him was not necessary to support their lifestyle, however he would need part-time employment to supplement that income. Pat had decided that a part-time position in the education industry would be a great fit for him.

In his mind that was the ideal and because of so many years of working in situations that were not ideal, he was not going to settle for anything less. I would continually remind Pat that he was not seeking a career in this part-time position. What he was seeking instead was financial stability and freedom to continue working on his new business.

Regardless over a 30-day period, Pat failed to see opportunities which presented themselves at least a half-dozen times. At networking events, individuals would ask Pat to send his resume, or randomly share an opening in their organization. Most of these opportunities were automatically written off because they were not in the education industry. For others he sat with the idea a few days but then determined the level of the position did not match where he was in his career.

Pat was seeking an opportunity that provided the financial security necessary to empower him to pursue his dreams. But his filters were limiting him to an opportunity that would provide fulfillment almost in lieu of his dreams.

We believe we can see everything that is happening in our lives so easily. What we fail to realize is how blind we have become. If we cannot even listen to the voice within ourselves, what makes us believe that we actually know what we are wandering around looking for?

I'm Still Wandering

Even though I have identified my purpose and am pretty clear on my passions, I still struggle to listen to the guiding voice within. I still doubt that it has my best interest in mind, and I still limit myself in many ways. The exercise I want to share with you for this lesson is one I use actively to this day. When I opened Leadership Arts Associates, I had no idea what I was doing, whether I could pull it off, or even what my organization was going to become. What I did know was that I was exactly where I needed to be at that moment. I knew this because I was utilizing this exercise to fully identify any opportunities that were present around me.

Of course nothing is foolproof. This exercise does not eliminate all our filters, however it drastically minimizes them. The intention of this exercise is to identify the most obvious opportunities that should not be missed.

The Rule of Three

This exercise is more of a practice for habitual change. It is recognizing that when someone or something is presented to you three times or more that you must explore it further. It does not dictate that you must commit to whatever this thing is, but only that you must at least explore it.

Sometimes you will notice a person who is presented to you three times, but you haven't got a clue about the possible relation or even how to approach them to explore it further. Believe me, I have been there... and I continue to be there. In fact, I have one situation right now where something is going on number five or six, yet I haven't gotten a clue on how to approach it. In some scenarios, the answer will come later, helping you to just approach it.

My family now attends services regularly at a large community church with multiple pastors. I absolutely love attending. I find the messages to be powerful and exactly what I need to hear at the moment. As typical, members always gravitate or prefer one pastor's style of teaching over the others and mine was Pastor Aaron. The way he structured his sermons and the messages he felt compelled to share simply struck a chord in my soul, time and time again. Despite this connection, I had never interacted with him personally.

The church is a very large congregation and I was perfectly comfortable being one in the sea of heads attending service. Then the rule of three kicked in. It started with randomly seeing Pastor Aaron at a retail store. I remember turning down an aisle and thinking, *Oh look, there's Pastor Aaron,* and continuing on my day. The second time was at church, I had somehow found my way to a hallway I was not familiar with and when I paused to look around and orient myself, I was standing in front of an office door with the name "Pastor Aaron." Finally, one day I was late for church because I wasn't feeling the best and decided to stop at an urgent care clinic before service. The parking lot was full and as a result I had to park way in the back. Another car pulled in right beside me. We exited our vehicles at the same time and there was Pastor Aaron. He said a very friendly good morning before proceeding towards the building. I said good morning back but inside knew that this was signal number three.

Being able to schedule a meeting with a pastor isn't hard – you simply send an email saying you'd like to talk and magically you are on their schedule. I remember being a little freaked out when I entered the church and he popped his head out of his office. "Oh hey Samm, come on in." How did he know who I was? Later, I found out he engages in his own personal practice of doing a quick look-up on Facebook just to familiarize himself with faces.

Pastor Aaron was the first person I articulated my Rule of Three to, because for the first time, I was unsure how to approach the person I'd been directed to. In this scenario, I told him my rule, told him our three encounters and then said, "Here I am."

I was surprised to learn that the opportunity presented to me from Pastor Aaron was a support I didn't know I was missing... and one that I much needed. Up until that point I had treated my faith as I did church service – fulfilling, but at a distance. That was intentional because I feared judgment. I was dealing with worthiness doubts that were so loud and so frightening. Pastor Aaron provided me the opportunity to create a relationship with God by simply extending the invitation. To date, I have only met with Pastor Aaron twice. At the end of each conversation he always says, "I'm not sure I've helped." I always chuckle inside because our conversations have such an impact on me that I am moved to tears even as I reflect back.

THE POWER OF YES

The advanced version of this exercise is one that most are not comfortable with. I am still not comfortable with it yet either. Nevertheless, I have experienced its valuable outcomes enough that I am willing to push through the discomfort. When you are ready, consider adding the practice of saying yes to the opportunities that are presented as an outcome of exploring the Rule of Three. For me it has included board opportunities, speaking engagements, new hires, or just staying in contact (which was Pastor Aaron's request). These opportunities present themselves for a reason, sometimes to help us grow, and in other circumstances to gain a new sense of clarity and direction.

THE DISCLAIMER

These opportunities push us to grow but are not all puppy dogs and rainbows. These are not invitations to your happily-ever-after. Sometimes the outcomes suck. Part One was full of them for me. I said yes to opportunities that resulted in pain. Still, it was that pain that brought forth healing which made me who I am today, with no regrets. This is where I believe the following mantra is applicable and full of truth: *What doesn't kill you, makes you stronger.*

COMPLETING THIS LESSON:

- Use your journal to record every time a person, place, or thing shows up at least twice.
- Continue recording instances as these people, places, and things show up.
- Say yes!
- In your journal, write any thoughts, feelings, wants, or needs that you have as a result of experience the rule of three.

Doreen
Samm
Shelly
Rhoda
Greg Bean

CHAPTER 14

In This Lesson, We Will:

- Discuss how life is full of lessons and we should strive to ultimately learn them in the moment
- Establish a practice to begin working on the skillset that will empower you to learn the lessons in the moment

Estimated Time to Complete this Lesson: 90 Days - 1 Year

Exposing Power

The power I am referencing here is not one from a place of ego but rather a place of peace. Life is messy, chaotic, and uncontrollably fast. In order to hear the guidance which comes from within, we must find a way to be still, quieting the noise that surrounds us constantly.

We must intentionally choose to craft our skill and our ability to tune in internally and tune out to external expectations of us. We must recognize the happenings of life for what they really are – lessons in growth. The ultimate goal is to be able to recognize this in the moment when it is happening. That is a complete separation from every protective system and reflex that kicks in as a response to the unknown.

In Chapter 7, I shared an experience that was so radical, I was almost in a state of disbelief that it was happening. It was an experience which should have easily triggered every protective system in my body. I don't think anyone would have deemed it unreasonable if the outcome at minimum had been some sort of verbal altercation. Yet the only protective system it activated was System Mama Bear – priority number one, protect my young – while the rest of me was left exposed and challenged to be curious about what that moment had to teach me.

I Noticed You Noticing Me

The exercise for this lesson is a practice. It is a skill set which must be developed. Without practice it will prove worthless in your development. This has been an exercise I have actively engaged in, albeit unknowingly, for most of my life, primarily because of my introverted nature. The ability to observe and take in, when presented with loud circumstances, is a lot like this exercise. The only difference is this exercise makes that innate behavior purposeful. If you struggle to observe and take in, know that this exercise might need to become your best friend if you desire to expose this power. But trust, such practice does consistently pay dividends, and one day, probably when you least expect it, it will click.

That is what happened to me in that radical experience. The practice finally clicked. I was able to learn the lesson about myself in the moment as it was happening, rather than engaging in the extremely tempting game of blame, passing judgment through my personal filter of why that person was not worthy of my time or attention – an easy write-off to avoid a lesson that is so uncomfortable and vulnerable in nature.

In moments where we have this part of ourselves held up for judgment, we cannot begin to process it, because we aren't even really sure what that part of our identity looks like. This response is not isolated to just motherhood or parenting. I think it can apply to those promoted to leadership positions. I think this applies to friendships, as well as every other relationship we build.

When and where are we given the opportunity to process our new identities as these titles and responsibilities are given to us?

PRACTICE MAKES PROGRESS

The following steps share the practice which should be utilized to work toward your ability to learn lessons about yourself in the moment that they are occurring. In order to do this, the practice will be centered around circumstances which are not directly related to you. The hope is, if no instant personal connection can be made, the likelihood of your personal protective systems being triggered will be drastically decreased. But understand, a part of this practice is that a personal connection will be established, despite how irrelevant the conversations appear. So it is important to maintain self-awareness and watch for when your protective systems are being triggered. This is critical because depending on when and how they are triggered, it could impact your outcomes, make the entire practice more challenging, or make it altogether ineffective.

Also, the steps below are designed to build upon each other. What this means is do not be afraid, or discount yourself, if a slower approach feels more your speed. Take your time and master step one before moving on to steps two and so forth. This is a skill set which must be developed over time, so racing to the finish line will only be a disservice to yourself.

To help with these steps, I have created downloadable coaching audio tracks (available at: sammsmeltzer.com/book).

STEP ONE. QUIET THE MIND

Select a practice environment of your choice. Find a place in nature, a bench at the mall, a seat in a café, or even your office. The only requirement is that motion of some sort must be happening around you and it must be a place where you will not be interrupted.

Close your eyes and bring your attention to your natural breath. On every exhale, attempt to push the noise which is populating your mind out. With every inhale, take in the sound that surrounds you. Continue this until the soundtrack of your surroundings is crystal clear, to the point that the sounds could paint a picture in your mind. Fully take in the soundtrack for at least 2-5 minutes.

STEP TWO. I NOTICE YOU

After mastering step one, you are ready to add visual aids. For step one, eyes remain closed because we are limiting the amount of stimuli that could trigger your personal protective systems. As you adapt to each level of stimuli, you'll add another. For this step, it will be to open your eyes.

Now, with the soundtrack of your surroundings so clear, notice what your vision adds. Where is your eye drawn? What colors stand out? What details in your surroundings catch your eye? What is the body language that now associates with some of the dialogue you potentially overheard?

For one client who was a Financial Advisor, this was the particular skill that allowed her to tune into prospective clients in random places throughout her day. One opportunity in particular that could be game changing to her career, was noticing people in a crowded diner as she ate tables away with her family.

STEP THREE. NOTICING ME

Trust your intuition. Believe that you have been intuitively guided to notice what you have noticed in this practice. Ask yourself, *"What does this have to do with me? Why am I noticing what I am noticing? What is the lesson that I must learn?"*

This lesson can be eye opening or cleverly subtle, but there will be a lesson.

"Overcoming the world is... a private, personal battle, requiring hand-to-hand combat with our own internal foes." – Neil L. Andersen

---

COMPLETING THIS LESSON:

- Practice Step One.
- Once Step One is mastered, begin practicing Step Two.
- After mastering Step Two, introduce Step Three.
- In your journal, write any thoughts, feelings, wants, or needs that you have after any time you complete this practice.

CHAPTER 15

EXPOSING MY HRART

When we started this journey together, I shared with you two interactions with writing coach and publisher, Demi Stevens, that led me to reach out and start writing this book. What I failed to share is that she was an opportunity as a result of the Rule of Three. My first connection with Demi was through a coaching client, though I didn't realize the connection was to Demi until later.

Lauren had come to me because she could feel her passion for her professional career fading. Through lots of work we discovered that Lauren had followed a professional path of offers. This meant that when someone offered her a job, she said yes and went with it. She was never given the opportunity to find her dream job or even identify what it could be. In our work, we discovered that her passion and dream was to write children's books. I can still remember her showing up for our sessions and when we talked about becoming an author her face would light up. She had found a Writer's Workshop being offered at a local venue and attended. That is when she met the writing coach and Demi fueled her dream in a way I never could. She made the dream possible.

Earlier I wrote about meeting Demi for the second time at a women's leadership event. When my friend and colleague, Amanda King released her book, that was my number three signal to create a connection with Demi. Whether I was ready or not, it was time to explore the opportunity... and with my yes philosophy, I said yes and never looked back.

SAMM THE AUTHOR

As I said before, I never intended to write a book. Sure, the idea of *Samm the author* sounded nice but also unrealistic. I wasn't a big reader and I was only a writer when required for educational or professional purposes.

In fact, when I finally decided to give in and write a book after several casual comments from others gently nudging that I should, I called Demi and I just blurted out whatever came to mind, because I didn't even know what the book I wanted to write was about.

At that point, I knew it would be easy to default to my professional HR and Training background and write a book filled with tips and lessons I've encountered over the years. That tome might still be in my future, but for my first book, it didn't feel right. For this first foray into writing, I wanted to share something that was vulnerable and heartfelt. I wanted to share something that was foundational.

The biggest difference between my work in the corporate world and the work I have been able to do as a third-party consultant is I have pushed for that readiness. Most of my work now is helping individuals get ready for success, to help them prepare for their purpose. This readiness varies from a simple shift in perspective to a full-on awakening in belief.

From the very beginning, I knew the stories I wanted to share. I knew the experiences that had happened to me that needed to be in this book. They were some of the most challenging realizations I have had to date. These realizations were hard lessons about myself that were necessary for me to grow. These lessons were my foundation, a starting place to begin moving forward on a path that I could take with newfound confidence.

This book was filled with heart from day one. In fact, it has transformed so much of my work. By providing the clarity I needed to understand that my work is heart work, I adapted this play on words by spelling heart as HRart. It's a combination of my HR background, my roots, and Leadership Arts Associates. But it is so much more to me than a play on words. HRart to me is purpose, passion, people, possibility, and power. These 5 P's manifest as 5 beliefs when it comes to my work as an HR Practitioner.

1. *I am a Human Resources Practitioner who helps individuals believe they have a purpose.*

They have a purpose in our organizations, they have a purpose in life.

2. *I am a Human Resources Practitioner who helps individuals find their passion and once it is found I help them find ways to keep that fire burning brightly.*

3. *I am a Human Resources Practitioner who is devoted to people, recognizing that they are the number one asset of any organization. I also recognize that they are people with a diversity that needs to be fostered.*

4. *I am a Human Resources Practitioner who believes in possibilities, in dreams, in visions, and in our ability to make them happen.*

5. *I am a Human Resources Practitioner who believes in power – an empowerment so strong and true that individuals bring their authentic voice to our organizations being aligned with our vision and values.*

Connecting with our people is the future of the HR industry and if this mindset is not embraced by organizations then I feel called to equip individuals with the ability to be at their absolute best.

That is what this book is all about: empowering you to work, live, and love all that you do.

"If we find ourselves with a desire that nothing in this world can satisfy, the most probable explanation is that we were made for another world." ~C.S. Lewis

COMPLETING THIS LESSON

If you have been working through the exercises as instructed in Part Two, you now have a collection of journal entries. These journal entries have captured and hold the initial exposures for you. It is now your turn to continue that discovery.

Read your entries from start to finish, look for themes, read between the lines. Share them with a friend and have them provide insight on what they believe may be the *unsaid*.

Use this as the foundation for continued inward growth personally and professionally. Most importantly, be proud of what you have accomplished and your dedication so far.

This journey takes bravery and courage.

If you're still asking, "What's next? I want more," then recognize that this is your blank canvas and you are the artist. Not me.

Know in your heart this is the beginning of a beautiful story that is long overdue to be told. It is yours to share with the world, and if you want to share it with us, you can do so on social media using #myHRart.

I cannot wait to see your masterpieces.

ADDITIONAL RESOURCES

I have created an entire page of resources for you online at www.sammsmeltzer.com/book.

There you will find the following:

- Rollercoaster Reflection – Audio Track
- Rollercoaster Reflection – Video Sample
- TFWN Journaling Technique – Video Tutorial
- Inner Child, Inner Joy – Audio Track
- Seeing It – Video Tutorial
- Toleration Evaluation – Video Tutorial
- Toleration Evaluation – PDF Worksheet
- The Rule of Three Tracking – PDF Worksheet
- I Noticed You Noticing Me – Coaching Audio

ABOUT THE AUTHOR

Samm Smeltzer has set out on a unique journey to achieve the most effective style of management and leadership within the workplace. With over a decade of HR experience she has discovered the key to transformation lies in creative methods.

Samm's experience stems from serving as a HR Manager within two U.S.-based retail companies for several years, responsible for multiple store sites in various states. Prior to the creation of Leadership Arts Associates, Samm developed and implemented company-wide educational programs for leadership and staff at a large Central Pennsylvania Healthcare System. Samm has functioned as a consultant to enhance team and individual performance.

She is certified by the HR Certification Institute as a Professional in Human Resources (PHR) and by the Society for Human Resource Management as a SHRM-CP.

Her dedicated efforts resulted in multiple awards including 2013 Organizational Learning & Development Educator of the Year and Penn State's 2015 Outstanding Graduate Student in Training and Development.

Samm's experience combined with her desire to educate and engage others resulted in the creation of Leadership Arts Associates, a firm devoted to revolutionizing professional and organizational development.

She is the proud wife of Josh and the mother of two little girls, Maddy and Zoey.

Made in the USA
Middletown, DE
20 January 2018